LAUREN W. WESTERFIELD

DEPTH

CONTROL

ESSAYS AND AUTOFICTIONS

UNSOLICITED
PRESS
PORTLAND, OREGON
SINCE 2012

Attention schools and businesses: for discounted copies on large orders,
please contact the publisher directly.

For information contact:
Unsolicited Press
Portland, Oregon
www.unsolicitedpress.com
orders@unsolicitedpress.com
619–354–8005

Cover Design: Kathryn Gerhardt
Editor: Summer Stewart

ISBN: 978-1-956692-94-5

This is a work of creative nonfiction, generously defined. As in, fictions permeate the memories, bodies, stories, textures, and names described herein. One might call these autofictions. Or one might call them casualties of human fallibility, of memory. Suffice is to say, once upon a time, they were inspired by a version of the truth.

CONTENTS

"My name, my body. Such versions, I occupy."

~Bhanu Kapil

"…my body does not have the same ideas I do."

~Roland Barthes

DEPTH
CONTROL
ESSAYS AND AUTOFICTIONS

INDENTATIONS

What I know is smaller than you'd think: my finger
when I touch the moon-chewed driftwood on my desk.
A single lemon seed, forgotten in a cup. Maybe you can't see this.
Like I said, it's small—small and intricate, which is to say,
the truth. People often think that truth is vast: untenable,
like love or god or sungold desert. People are wrong about this.
You, I think, are wrong. You aren't looking
close enough. I am asking—
and when I say *you*, I might be speaking to my finger as it reaches,
stretching down the hollow cup-neck darkness.
Or I might be speaking to the fingers of a former lover
as he passes me outside the window of a coffee shop, or grips
the flesh around my hipbones in the sweatdrip of last summer.
Or I might be speaking to the fingers of a lover who is very new:
to red and rust, patterning the sheets after he reaches,
stretches up inside. Sometimes I'm no bigger than a question,
than a finger, than an eyeball, than a bite mark, than a voice
wrapped up in all of you [seawood, citrus, bone]. This
is what I'm trying to explain: how slippery it is—you are—
and why, eventually, we find ourselves un-soggy, first, then dry.
Forgotten in our dailiness, and every night, the moon

making another hungry pass. This is how it always goes.
What I know is true [the way this water on my tongue
and now my throat and my esophagus and trickling between my ribs
is true]: that when I said I would still love you for a while,
I was both lying
and confessing. And what of it? What does it matter
if tonight the moon is full, its body stretched and eight-limbed
like a spider, and the sidewalk sweats with new May heat, and you
are in an airplane heading south over the moonrise hills, and I
am in a short red dress you loved once, slipped once
up over my thighs and belly skin, slipped the flowers
and the cotton up and up but not all the way off
and fucked me fast and scared the cat? What does it matter
if you loved me once, and once upon a time last May
you were again boarding a plane? Or maybe you:
who so often left me without leaving,
your body always running warm,
your eyes forever fixed upon the stars? Or you,
who sits beside me even now, your closeness like a postcard,
your absence hovering between us like a breath?
It matters because of this *again*. Because the pattern is a wave.
Because the pattern is a river. Because the pattern
is a hidden cove receding from a shore
that I have never seen and always known. I say again [nearly:
to a quick-fuck afternoon in May, to a red dress or your hands]
—but you would say that isn't how it works. And I would say
that you are wrong. This is what *I* know. This is how *I* work.

Suppose I wandered back into *again*
and counted every lemon that you bought because I told you
that I liked them, squeezed and dropped into hot water
in the morning. Every seed caught waterlogged and left
to crack-dry in the sink. Suppose I wandered back into *again*
and wondered at this hunger: what drives the biting—wanting—
yours, and mine? Suppose I counted off the letters
of the alphabet: A, then B, then C, and then—?
Suppose I wandered back to pick the lock that keeps me
separate from you [no matter how conjoined our bodies
might have been some nights and mornings:
wet and stuck so close that no air could get through,
or wet and bleeding on the white sheets of your strange white bed,
or dry and slick just like a dream birth, like a pearl].
Suppose I recognize how much I have resisted this—containment—
even as I hunger[ed] for your arms [a box]
to crawl inside. And then suppose I say: this is not about you.
You might think I'm lying. You would be wrong.
This is not about the *you* you think you know—the you
of two strong wrists and thinning hair, three tattoos and one
weak heart. Or you of poetry and sea glass eyes, of menthol
and my favorite hands. Or you of hair so long and black
and heavy like a funeral, soft palms brown and laced
with sweat. Or even you: as in, the you of me:
of here and now and lip-bit thought, of flitting hands
and bony shoulders, bloodshot eyeballs, tongue tracing
the outline of night-bludgeoned teeth. Not as such.

What I mean to say: this is not about your body.
Later, there will be nothing left.
I am trying to explain. All the yous inside of me—
voices, fingers, citrus, teeth—
and how they touch. How they beckon and recede. How they bite
into the weave of me, then stick.
I want to talk about your body as a mordant form.
About components—yours and mine [fingers, forearms,
tattoos, lemons, sea glass, cat hair]and how they constitute
a frame. A pattern [box]: nesting all of you and me and us inside.
Something to contain the things I've come to know
or want to. All the small things that are true.
All the small things that are true again. It isn't easy.
Not like orange pith, or greengold
prairie hills in springtime, or a quick red dress.
The truth is more like reaching: as I run my finger
down the dishsoap-slick ceramic, groping for the seed.
Or else it is the want. I want to know—
want someone to want to know about the seed.

I.

MADONNA OF THE MASTER BATH

Fall is coming. I find myself walking past East City Park, daydreaming of trouser socks. A hot Americano in a blue ceramic cup. This morning, I am working from my desk. The leaves outside my window have begun to turn, but in a way that seems unnatural—as in, burnt orange at the edges due to heat and smoke, in this sense literally *burnt*. They rustle: the sound a crispness more like crumpled paper than North Idaho in autumn.

Inside the window: on the ledge above my books, one air plant is thriving. The other is quite dead. I haven't thrown it out yet—less because I have some hope of its return than because it was a gift from a friend who has since moved to Seattle, and the little gold-ridged pot reminds me of her.

Re-potting isn't like me. I have the most un-green of thumbs. Still, something about today and this new nearly-autumn-almost-chill moves my fingers into weak and skinny roots, into rocks and dirt, until the last gasp of air plant—browning, limp—falls into the trash. In its place, I scoop the little body of a succulent I'd purchased—frivolously, earnestly—at a writing residency in Port Townsend, Washington, last summer. The same residency where

I'd met the friend who gave me the now indecorously interred air plant.

Yesterday I broke my favorite green wine glass in the sink.
It seemed like it should be bad luck, but then the day was rich.
I am not a very superstitious person—but suddenly, I wonder
                                            about breaking other things.

~ ~ ~

Several weeks ago, I went to the dentist to pick up a night guard: clear plastic apparatus molded in the same shape as my gums and teeth. To stem the grinding—finally, at thirty-two, after several years' suggestion. At first, I did not make the connection: the way the dreams unfurled darker, stranger, once I started wearing it to bed—

> [Inside: men and doors and threesomes that I do not want to be a part of, someone leaving for bananas, apples, condoms. You are also there. This is both a comfort and a horror. You are on the phone, then in the shower, telling everyone about the threesomes and the fruit. Next, an older student reaches out, his fingers, rubs my shoulder, seizes the fabric of my shirt, the collar. You are there and you are not there—]

All of this revolves around my body. This dream, the narrative, too vivid, bright—more real than bone. Teeth are barriers. My mind assaults the bone to keep from feeding on itself. Plastic does not work the same. The dentists warned me: this thing inside my mouth won't stop the grinding. It only mitigates the damage. I do not want to lose my teeth. I also do not know if he and I share understandings of this word: DAMAGE.

~ ~ ~

Evening. A chill that hits my shins. Skips the ampleness of thigh, then centers, pinned, against mid-spine. Spreading like white paint along each rib-cage wing.

I receive a text from B—the ex who now lives down the hall, who is now my neighbor—to say that he's left wine outside the door. I didn't ask for wine. I asked for packing tape. This is because he is my neighbor, and we are trying to be friends, and I didn't want to buy a roll of tape just to return these sunglasses that looked elegant online but look bad against my face. It has been almost exactly seven months since we broke up. I say as much via text—that is, about the tape; not about the glasses, or my face, or passing time. I say as much, and within minutes he is at my door, packing tape in one hand and his tiny blue-gray cat against his shoulder.

He knows I will invite them both to come inside [I do] and let her explore and sniff my furniture, my walls, my books [I do]. We talk about the tasting at the wine shop where he works, about the fruity nose on this year's vintage of a stalwart Côte du Rhône. We watch the cat explore my closet, crevices behind the bed, beneath the couch. She saves the bed itself for last, makes as if to settle, then shifts her attention to the windowsill and perches there instead, observing from the inside out.

~ ~ ~

Once, when I was young, I dreamt I gave birth to a cat. I was fourteen, and I was inside the dream, which happened in my brain, inside my body.

[Inside: I was wearing this electric coral dress. It was a long dress, from the '70s, a disco vibe in heavy polyester with a cutout belly, patterned, woven loops and mesh and showing skin without the skin, a hint without the *actual* of skin. I was fourteen and my hair was brown and long and I was tall already for my age but still not quite grown *in* (to ears and nose and bangs and wisdom teeth never erupted, not yet pulled) and I was so, so calm. I can remember this distinctly. Everything about the inside of this—dreaming, body, birth--I can remember. How I walked up just three stairs into my parents' then-bedroom. Walked into their

master bathroom, closed the sliding door, moved
the whole time like a woman older than I was,
somebody worldly, with secrets. How I closed the
sliding door and went inside and when I opened it
again, it turns out, I had given birth. As in, I went
inside the inside of the inside of my mind and
there, it seems, I had been pregnant. Invisibly—no
straining on the fabric of the belly mesh, the loops,
the heavy polyester—but nevertheless, a mother
(nearly). I gave birth to a cat. This was, inside the
inside of the thing—the dream, my mind, my
body—utterly un-strange. I was so calm. I looked
beatific: odd Madonna of the master bathroom
and the Russian Blue, a smile on my lips, the black-
blue-gray of cat (not kitten but a full-grown cat—
this seems important) huddled whole and gorgeous
at my coral breast]

~ ~ ~

Saturday. You and I. We meet downtown. We walk the Farmer's
Market. Get coffee. After two full years of friendship, and now two
hot summer months of something we're not quite sure how to
name, this is the closest to a date we've managed yet. It is a perfect,
yellow-gold, September kind of day. We decide to hike.

Stickers from the tall dry grass, clinging to my socks. The very fact
of socks at all; remembering to bring a sweater; autumn. Even this

seems resonant, somehow. The season. Change, and chill. You throw a leaf against the slime-green film of—what is it, anyway? Algae? Stagnant green that coats this silent pond, keeps the surface still—and nothing moves. You crouch to take a photograph, analog, black & white film, your father's camera. You tell me stories of your father, of your mother, how they met. We walk in no particular direction.

I stand a bit behind and take a photograph of you.

Earlier, you took several of me. I'm never quite sure what to do with my hands in photographs that are supposed to be candid but aren't. I wonder if you will develop them. If the black & white will pick up, as you say, all the shadows crossing over shades of brown and gold. September on the Palouse prairie. How you will remember me inside the photograph:

[flannel, turquoise, wind]

～～～

Cats have sharp little teeth.

I do not have a cat of my own. But I have welcomed marks—small rounds, surface punctures—along the skin between my thumb and index finger. The gnaws that sweet-hurt—that I often wish would stay until the morning. There is a pull, an almost-eroticism, about the challenge, and subsequent pleasure, of earning [winning?] intimacy with other people's cats.

Especially men.

Especially lovers.

Correction. The qualifier was a lie. I know it, even as I write the words. These bites, the marks, aren't *almost* erotic. Do I seek them out? These men with cats? The pleasure of the not-quite-puncture? The flash of skin or hurt or in-between-ness that is *toothmarks*, that is *not my cat*, that is *seduction*, that is *the space between, before*—

[an indentation]

Cats can only move their jaws up and down, up and down. Not side-to-side. Hence the puncture; little sweet-hurt gnaw. A cat would not, could not, grind her teeth.

Perhaps, after all this, I'm just jealous.

What do cats dream? How? What if I am sleeping with a man, and that man's cat, and said cat crawls onto my chest or curls against my stomach or the sleep-droop of my thigh, and we are both asleep and dreaming, and she purrs or speaks or moves her teeth—

~ ~ ~

I tell you all about the cat-birth dream. I ask if I'd already told you once before. You say, in fact, I hadn't told you yet. About the dream. About the birth. About my love of polyester, and the fact that B's cat [or yours—we'll call you C—depending on the day, the twist and curl of time, of when I'm writing this, the skin of it, the taste of *you* against my lips and what it seems to mean] is also partly Russian Blue, is wholly small and gray and whole inside her smallness, seven pounds of small, and not a kitten even though he calls her one.

This seems important.

You and I, we talk about the tiny blue-gray cat. But then we stop. We've been friends too long, and by now you've already heard too much about B, about his cat. What I mean is this: it's too late now, for us—for you and me—to be sensitive, to have secrets, without lying. All that I can do is hold things back. We talk, but I don't tell you everything. I let the conversation swerve into this wondering: about the cat-birth dream, about cat dreams in general, and what they mean. Because we are alike in many ways, you look it up. You find a lot of vague and inconclusive information, verging on cliché: about how cats are instinctually feminine, independent, and aloof;

about how pregnancy dreams in those who aren't expecting have to do with anxiety around a project or decision, an effort towards "inner development." No one on the internet seems to have experience with dreams where human women bear full-grown cats instead of kittens. I don't say so, but I take some satisfaction in this—in my peculiarity, at fourteen; in my cat dream with a twist.

As if I could take credit.

What I also don't say is that now—because I'm sitting with you, sleeping with you—the catalog of things this dream could mean expands. Its insistence reaches into this: into you and I, into our present moment. Now the dream encompasses and echoes not only Russian Blue but also orange Maine Coon: twenty pounds and shedding all over my ankle socks and blouse, curled against my naked thighs inside my memory of summer, white sheets damp with sweat and stained and you, reading me to sleep with Stephen Dunn's *Loves*, waking me with you on one side, Maine Coon on the other, enveloped in a basement room that somehow stayed so cool long after August cooked the morning sun against the pavement.

Now the dream encompasses and echoes both of these, and more: the fact that *you* are you today—C—but once upon a time the *you* inside my mind was B, or even A, was simply *he*, or *she* [the blue-gray cat inside the inside of my dreaming teenage mind, inside my body]. That now there's *he* and *you* and *cat*, and everything is multiple—her teeth, the way her mouth will open with so little sound and just a flash of canine, just a hint of *speak* and *want* and

15

yes I know that it is you—still she bites at memory. Still, she winds her tiny body into mine.

~ ~ ~

The last time he left town, B gave me visitation rights, but not the key. This time, all of it—the cat, the key, the half-full bottle of Rioja from another tasting—curls into a single, slender olive branch. I do not tell you this. I keep meaning to, but then I don't. What would it accomplish? It's not as if I owe you this particularity of truth [that is, not exactly; not when we aren't calling ourselves anything, when what we say most of the time is that we probably should stop, that we are equally unready to invest, to do right by one another—], and no other reason seems quite good enough. Every justification I can think of pretends to be about transparency but ends up [if I'm honest with myself] being about power.

I do not want this to be true.

So all I tell you is that B and I are trying to be friends. That we have tried before and failed. I leave out my late-night visits to his dark apartment—visits where I pet the cat, and throw her silly little toys around, and hold her close, and sniff her fur until she wriggles free; visits where I sip a glass of wine, and look inside B's fridge, his cupboards, and eat a covert potato chip, perhaps, the way I used to when I had permission. I leave out how the cat [and to a lesser extent, the wine] is something of a crux, a gauge, between us.

Gauge = standard of measure [also sounds like *gouge*—just one letter different—that is, "a chisel with a concave blade; an indentation or a groove made by gouging; or, to swindle."From the Old Welsh *gylph*, "a beak, or pointed instrument."]

You and I are up late, writing. I ask you how to spell *gouge*. In the moment, as I look it up, I am forgetting. My eyes are tired, my contact lenses dry and sticking, and I should have thought to take them out, to wear my glasses. We are sitting at the bar as I am writing this, mining definitions, iterations. You are writing poems. You say *g-o-u-g-*, and I am off, on the hunt. Hoping to find inside the thing I want to find—reference to an indentation or a tooth, and so I do, and so I laugh and slap the blonde wood of the table, then apologize immediately.

I know why, and I don't know why.

Sorry. Such a damning, constant word.

You remind me of the time, earlier this summer, when you told me to look up *bight*—a bend or curve inside a coastline, oftentimes recessed. I remember that I did; I remember to remember how it resonates: with me, with bite, with toothmarks, with my gums and with the water near the piece of California land where I was born.

~~~

My teeth are sensitive to sweetness, tart, and ice.

What I haven't said, straight out: the why of it. That is, why it ended between B and I. As far as I can tell, it was my mind. Not *in* my mind, but actually my mind itself. The fact and curl of it. The way it funnels to my lips in waves and torrents, like a beach storm, and the torrents shoved and pummeled him, and he has always been, still is, so very much from the Midwest; so completely land bound. He once told me: *you say a lot of things when you talk.* He wasn't wrong. After about a year, he stopped wanting to keep track. He told me: *sometimes I just can't.*

It's hard to hold the choice against him. What I resented was the bait and switch: the way he started off enamored of my mind, then changed his own—decided, after all, that spending time with mine was too much work. Then again, inside a busy mind is not an easy place to be, and when the wind is clicking through the drying yellow leaves outside my window on an autumn morning, I feel soothed; but how was he supposed to know about all that?

To be fully seen and known, by a mind as hungry and as curious: this is not a slight demand. And I was not only demanding; I was careless. I failed to consider what it was I wanted relative to whom I was asking—failed, that is, to consider what my therapist might call "matters of capacity." Failed to consider: if I wanted what I wanted from the man I had, or from a fiction of a man, or truly, underneath it all, from just myself.

B used to say, half-mockingly, half-troubled: *I can't read your mind. You can't expect me to.* I used to laugh, then nod. I'd say, *Of course. Don't be silly. I would never.* This was a lie. I never told him what I used to tell my friend S—as she and I would talk, and drink our half-price Tuesday wine at the otherwise expensive restaurant on the corner, the restaurant with warm lighting and red brick and pretty window-walls so people walking by could see us from the outside in; as she and I would sit there in our nearly-matching jeans and soft black sweaters, splitting a plate of Spanish olives, wondering if it's even possible to live inside a woman-body and ever *not* feel like an object in the world—that secretly, I did expect it. That secretly, foolishly, I thought one's close attention could be like clairvoyance. S understood; but I worried B would not. So I never told him this until the end. Until we were unraveling. I suspect it frightened him. It frightened me as well: because, for several months, I'd been unhappy, crying often, feeling anxious, hating how he kept on telling me to *just relax, be easy.* It frightened me because, before all this, I'd been in love with someone else, with A, and so soon after that I'd met B. I'd wondered, and I'd wavered, and I'd caved; and then, so quickly, I'd demanded knowingness from him, from someone new.

What I mean to say is this: What if he had given it?

What I mean to say is, I'd been so busy wanting to be seen that I, myself, lost sight.

~ ~ ~

Once, you asked me: *who are you, lying naked in a field?*

I loved the question but did not know the answer.

I replied: *I'm scared. I'm scared. Unless I am a child, or inside a dream.*

~ ~ ~

What shape are we—now, tonight?

An orange cat, more creamsicle than orange, tufts of hair that shed and ball on contact, somehow, even just in passing, and a purr that rumbles through this studio apartment—even pit against this sound of autumn breeze, the bass line thumping from downstairs, a restaurant closing soon and kitchen staff are turning up the volume. You and I are sitting, writing, talking [me more than you, which always renders me self-conscious: the way you then think I'm anxious, and I feel the way your thoughts are bending, and then I DO get anxious, and we sit and write and mostly it is good but all along there is this wire buzzing underneath the table—]

It is a new apartment [yours], and there are many new peripheries.

Scent of litter box, familiar. Tufts of cream and orange hair, increasingly familiar [but still less so than blue, than gray]. All the cabinets in your apartment have these funny latches on them— silver chrome, old-fashioned, noticeable against the bright white new of paint. You just moved in this week. I want to turn the latches, look inside the cupboards, know what kind of groceries you buy. I am a nosy person, curious. I know you are observant, so observant of me in particular—of my qualities, my tics, my would-be hiddens. Like the eye thing, darting up and to the right when I am nervous. How you noticed this before I noticed it myself, told me that you've noticed it for years. How I felt stripped down in the best way when you said it—as in, naked; as in, known.

Somehow, I feel that you would not be bothered, might even be a little flattered, to indulge my prying.

But the latches trip me up. They refuse to open easily, the way a simple knob might open, and it slows my fingers—pull of curiosity, of *us-ness*—so I stop. We, too, say that we should stop. What reason, then, to turn the chrome a little harder? Exert the pressure of my fingers down and to the left? Crack open some new thing within the in-between that is the two of us?

~ ~ ~

Teeth.

I haven't worn the night guard for several weeks. Dreams come and go in strangeness. This morning, it is perfectly gray and rainy, just the right degree of rustle in the wet-bone branches. I want to hibernate. Curl in.

Porous boundaries plague me. Is this the converse of feeling like an object? Is feeling like an object always bad? Like a cat, her jaw confined to nothing but *up-down, up-down.* How she doesn't even have the choice, the challenge not to grind—is this a limit, or a blessing?

I'm thinking that I wouldn't mind containment if it clarified divisions between *myself* and *other* [at least right now, this moment—this is how I feel this morning, why I didn't go to work today, why I didn't want to be another body in a room with other bodies]. But this becomes a problem if the container is created by somebody else. If I know its form and curl and edge too well.

~ ~ ~

Not long ago, I had a dream where I was lost inside my own apartment. In the dream, I was thirty-two. I was inside the dream, which happened in my brain, inside my body.

[Inside: I was trying to get back to my apartment but the building had grown infinitely long, and I was starting at the far end. Sunlight, bright like midday—except it was in fact around four in the morning. My colleague K from my graduate program was there and we exchanged pleasantries; she was wearing shorts and trying to find someplace to buy fruit juice. I went inside and climbed the stairs—broad, metal, industrial. I kept getting confused about which floor it was, and how to get back to my own. At times, the hallways in the building opened into arcade-like spaces: bright lights, whirring colors, games or slot machines. I wasn't particularly arrested by this, more annoyed by the sea of people and distraction. I was tired, and I wanted to go home. The building wouldn't end]

~~~

It's not the cat-birth aspect of the dream, per se, that I hold on to—that feels particular to me. When it comes to cat dreams, I know that I am one of many. S told me that she had a cat-birth dream, back when she was pregnant with her daughter. And just the other day, my colleague K told me how she dreamt that she was pregnant once—anxious, worried, only twenty-one—then ran into the ocean, stepped into the waves, and gave birth to a kitten. *I was so relieved,* she'd said. *I was like, 'YES.' Because a kitten was so small; it was something I could handle.* Even my own mother dreamt of kittens: at thirty-two, newly pregnant with me, she dreamt I came out small and black and feline; dreamt me into something utterly unlike the fat and red and angry, gasping, two-week-late, ten-pound baby-self that came instead, at last, when she was thirty-three.

It's not the cat-birth part that's odd. What's odd is how the cat was grown, and I was not. How whole and gorgeous her small cat-self was, and how her blue-gray hair shone sliver up against my coral dress. How some slight knowing still exists inside me, every time I think of this: that inside the inside of the dream, the two of us together—my grown baby-cat and I—rendered me impervious to stares and questions, to the gossip and the scrutiny I knew I'd face as soon as I stepped past the shower door, beyond the master bath and out into the world.

[THIS BODY] FICTIONS

I grew up playing dress-up. Three, four, five years old. Not with costumes—princess costume, fairy costume—but with thrifted chaos: pink tulle skirt, pink pith helmet, velvet stovepipe, cobalt kimono. There are photos of me, wrapped in mauve chiffon and my grandfather's butterscotch silk airman's scarf, dancing to Satie and Stravinsky on the Persian rug in our living room. Or painting with watercolors on the kitchen floor, dipping my paintbrush in a Star Trek coffee mug to wash it clean between strokes. There are home movies: me, legs splayed on brown and cream tile, chattering away. The words themselves are silly, strange—*blockies, plazy, fitch, glap*—but underneath them all, a sturdy confidence. Words and stories tumbling, rolling out from my small, rotund body, out from underneath my orange cotton dress, green leggings, pink helmet, floral scarf.

My mom had studied fine arts in college. She framed one of my paintings. It's an abstract mess: hot pink center, clumps of purple-red, and butter-yellow rising over everything. A kaleidoscope. I was an only child, frequently alone but rarely lonely. Looking at the painting now, I try to recall the thrill of feeling—anything, everything. Getting up at 6AM for cereal and toast because there were block cities to finish, drawings of "Princess Bat" and "King of the Mice" to color in, complete. Throwing paint on the page, tossing a cape over my shoulders, pulling a t-shirt up over my head and wearing it like a headdress as I spun in circles, over and over, until I collapsed into a heap.

Then I was nine, new in school, with ugly brown shoes. Mom had heard stories about the public middle school in our small bay-front refinery town: stories about sex and drugs and some girl who stabbed another girl with a pencil. She and Dad opted for the private catholic K-8 across the Carquinez Strait—the feeder school to something safer, more refined, the kind of place where girls wore tidy uniforms and everything was made of bright red brick. The feeder school itself was pale pink concrete, and the uniforms were ugly: blue and beige and polyester pleated slacks, long skirts, and thinly woven polo shirts.

I only had one friend there: another dancer, H, from ballet. We met when I was in the third grade, before I went to the new school. Our ballet classes were held in the old military barracks near the bay, in the shadow of the bridge. I'd been going there since I was two and a half years old, ever since I saw Mikhail Baryshnikov in the 1977 production of *The Nutcracker* on PBS and danced around the den in my polyester nightgown to the music. H came much later. She was the new girl in class. We wore matching black bell skirts with multicolored trim during dance lessons, then went over to her house and played make believe out in the yard. At my old school, I had lots of friends. But H was the first one I loved. She was petite and lithe and had the best kind of scrunchies. I found her beautiful.

Soon, H and I were best friends. I was always going over to her house to play and spend the night. We would spend the afternoons clambering amongst the rocks by the bay, pretending we were Nancy Drew and George Fayne, searching for evidence and writing down "clues" in Disney Princess pocket diaries with tiny copper locks built in. When she came to my house, we would dress up in thrifted gowns from the Goodwill Store and prance around the yard, then make lemonade from scratch in the sunset of the kitchen.

Then we each turned ten. It was fifth grade. In ballet, H got cast as Clara in *The Nutcracker*. I got cast as a mouse. H got a boyfriend and her period, and I got neither. My mother wouldn't let me shave my legs, and meanwhile H's legs were always smooth, and her hair was always bouncing, bouncing. I watched her on the playground at recess, laughing over the latest episode of *Friends* with two other pretty girls—one redhead, one blonde—all in their matching skirts and white sneakers. My mother wouldn't let me watch *Friends* because of all the sex, or so she said, and my shoes were weird dark brown leather ergonomic oxfords. H and I both had brown hair, and mine was arguably shinier but had absolutely zero bounce. Back then, it was the bounce I wanted. Without it, I sat alone in the shade of the picnic benches during recess. H stopped calling, stopped coming over to do homework or make lemonade, stopped inviting me to spend the night.

So I brought books with me to lunch. I watched H and her new best friends, and I read things, and I felt the urge to change. To be someone other than myself: this body, too tall for my age, with big feet and brown shoes, sitting alone on the bench with a tartan lunch box and cartons of soymilk and carrot sticks and peanut butter sandwiches. Of course, none of these were qualities of selfhood, not really. My actual self unfurled when I was alone, or in my head. I still played dress-up, played soccer because I loved to run, kept going to ballet because I loved the music and the movement and (not that I would have said it this way, because I didn't even learn the word until the sixth grade, but) fuck being Clara in *The Nutcracker*, because what mattered to me back then was the wearing tights and listening to Tchaikovsky and jumping around. But by the time I was ten, jumping around wasn't good enough anymore. Not for traveling team. Not for going on pointe. Not for serious players, dancers. At first, I didn't care. Then I learned that not caring came with a price. I got left behind. I lost things.

That is when the game of dress-up changed. I started dressing up with purpose—a way to practice being something, or someone, else. At school, I was studious and quiet. I wore my uniform and my ugly brown shoes and my brown hair tied back with no bounce, no scrunchie, just those straight-across bangs that my mom cut herself over the bathroom sink. 11, 12, 13 years old. At home, I tried new identities on for size. I would sit at my desk doing my homework, a backdrop from all the books I'd read filling my mind, pretending that my suburban bedroom was one of Forester's naval ships, or Austen's estates, or a hacienda on the old El Camino Real. At night, before going to bed, I would put on my old dress-up clothes from Goodwill, then teeter across the carpet in my mother's patent leather pumps. I would stand before the bathroom mirror, practice raising one eyebrow, imagine making arch comments to a room filled with 19th century novel men, daring them to charm me. Daring them, that is, to try—making them earn it. This was imperative, although I wasn't yet sure why. All I knew was this: it was part of something larger. Something I had gleaned about the ways that sex and power worked in tandem.

Then I'd kiss the molding on my closet door. Press my lips, in borrowed "Chinaglaze Red" Moondrops Lipstick by Revlon, up against the smooth white paint.

In high school, we learned to peel the body down. Peer inside the chest, inside the heart, and examine its functions. In class, the body was a science project. Everywhere else, it was a constant enigma. I was fourteen and lonely, and my nose was too big for my face. My own body was stretching, elongating the space between my feet and my hips, my heart and my brain. My period had gone quickly from an excitement to a burden to a betrayal. On the first day of school, I bled straight through my brand-new cream and yellow skirt while sitting in assembly. I spent the afternoon blushing, mortified, a sweatshirt tied around my waist.

In Honors Biology, we broke the body into modules and systems: circulatory, respiratory, skeletal, sensory. We learned that the body is highly organized. I tried to take comfort in the structure. I clung to the notion of this paper body, even as my own became that much harder to control. According to my textbooks, the paper body was balanced. Its functions and behaviors were mapped out, every spurt and secretion imbued with purpose. I learned that the paper heart operates on four chambers and two valves, with pipes running through each side to draw blood in, to pull blood out. I learned that pumping is the heart's sole purpose. That it keeps things in check, keeps time like a soldier, marches to a steady one-two count: *lubb-dupp*.

This wasn't how it worked at all when the boy I liked—a boy who was a friend, who talked to me often but flirted with other girls, a boy whose charm had me on the phone all night with my girlfriends, swooning—walked past me in the hall, or sat beside me in AP U.S. History, or asked to borrow my pencil during a quiz in Italian II. Not even remotely. But I learned to push the heat, the thumping, further down. I was a smart girl. All the teachers and the mothers said so. They made it clear: this body, its rebellions, were distracting. This body was the kind of thing that boys could sniff and hear, echoing against the lockers. Or so my mother, and my friends' mothers, and my 19th century novel-fed imagination had led me to believe. Bodies were dangerous. Bodies got girls into trouble. I believed, almost hoped, that this was true. Because, as much as I wanted to be "good" and "smart," I also wanted, someday, to be wanted. That these options were not mutually exclusive beyond the realm of fiction hadn't yet occurred to me. I was a good close reader. I thrived on subtext. *Northanger Abbey* and *Jane Eyre* gave me goose bumps, and I delighted in their gothic excesses; clung to the promise that good girls might one day stumble into a romantic story and get swept off their feet. The possibility that I would find a "nice man," as the mothers liked to say—but also, along the way, several bad ones. Men who would teach me things.

The question was: what things? What did *wanting* even mean for me—inside my life, my body?

At school, I had a full AP schedule and a 4.0+. I only got calls from boys who wanted help with their homework. I got calls from *that* boy and would stay up at night on the phone with him, just us two alone in the dark, discussing the ramifications of the Marshall Plan while I closed my eyes and imagined him telling me other things entirely, my cheek shoved up against the closet door molding.

DEPTH CONTROL

Graduation came. I went to college. Northern California to Vermont. 3,000 miles between my past and my future: a future without uniforms or curfews. A tiny liberal arts college with no Greek system, no big city nearby, lots of blue-gray marble buildings and excuses to wear stocking caps and glasses and moth-eaten sweaters from the thrift store. In college, I dressed up for real. I dyed my hair red, donned a costume of black turtlenecks and black eyeliner. I drank lots of black coffee. I ditched the 19th century melodrama and picked new poets—scribes I could wear on my sleeve without (I thought) giving my heart away. My new canon was Kerouac, Olson, Spicer. I copied their staccato. I tried to spend more time thinking about jazz and sex and art. These things seemed far from gothic. This seemed like a safer brand of romance—post-19th century-novel-men, post-palm-sweats, post-modern. Listening to Miles, listening to Mingus, I'd think back to driving through Big Sur with open windows, salted air, and reconceive my memory: add a soundtrack, add a lover, stick a fictive spliff between my teeth.

In college, there were many boys who pretended to be men. These men, these characters, fit my newfound script. Book-smart men. Smooth talkers. Older men, like my friend's brother of high school football fame and fancy vodka, Harvard degree and a loft in the city, the one who invited me for drinks and dinner on the pier one summer night and touched my leg under the table, who made me feel powerful when I let him pay, let him kiss me, then left before anything more could happen between us. Or younger men, like my roommate's boyfriend's buddy of the southern drawl and nearly-see-thru charm, golf shirts and a second-shelf Syrah, the one who talked his way into my graces, who drew me in with easy banter and chaste kisses on the cheek, then vanished as soon as I kissed

21

I

him back. Men, in other words, who played dress-up like I did; who put on a worldly air and let me do the same as long as I could keep the upper hand. Who reminded me how the game worked if I slipped up—that is, started to believe them, or started to care.

So I played the game with caution. I kept reading. I kept sleeping alone—not because I wanted to, but because the alternative was still so risky; so totally unknown. I was afraid of what I'd lose.

In college, I learned that drinking was another kind of dress up. I'd pour a gin and tonic, or a coffee mug of Carlo Rossi, then turn up the Mingus, smudge some black stuff around my eyes, and let the alcohol settle in, slow my thoughts down, smooth the rough edges of my mind. With a drink in hand, I could believe my own imagined self was somehow real. That I was clever and flirtatious. That I could be anyone I wanted. I was Didion, or Kyger, or di Prima. And for a little while, it seemed, I could recapture that long-lost feeling of openness: a warmth in my limbs that made me less afraid to peel my body off the wall, to brush my skin against someone else's in the dark. That was the temptation, and the risk: the possibility of foreign touch. But most nights, I went home before anything could happen. I didn't have sex. I rarely kissed. Instead, I drank more wine. I smoked pot and listened to Tori Amos and Fiona Apple and read poetry to defuse the tension.

I saw my body in pieces then and imagined the center to be in my brain somewhere, up at the top. That was where I got off. It was where things made sense. I took Philosophy 101 and nodded along to Plato, to Aristotle, to notions of platonic dualism. This was logic, I thought. This separation of the body and the mind. This sense that the body as a safe and normal thing was something more like fiction. That the body, no matter how miraculous, was also always a liability.

My body mapped its route with bursts and palpitations. Its topography was one of unexpected detours, trembling fingers, unbidden teeth, rare peace in the throat. This was true whether I was alone or not. Whether I was being or pretending. I would still play dress-up. I would stain my lips a bitten red, and wear cheap blush called "Orgasm." It was easy—as easy as five dollars and a nearby Walgreens. But ease, I'd come to learn in time, was not the same as authenticity. Was not even the same as wanting or desire.

I had sex for the first time when I was 22. It was a calculated move. The concept of virginity had turned on me, morphed from Catholic schoolgirl virtue to a kind of bait. I—that is, my body— had become a prize. My virginity, a trophy. I wanted to be rid of it—not lose it, as the saying goes, so much as neutralize its potency.

The boy I chose was neither tall nor clever. He was not the boy I thought I loved. He was neither blonde, nor funny, nor from California. He didn't read Ken Kesey or share my love of yellow mustard. He didn't read much of anything. Perhaps most importantly, he did not possess that critical brand of charm: the kind that H had wielded over me so many years before, the kind that I sensed in this blonde surfer boy from Redondo Beach who loved mustard and Kesey and told me I was beautiful but clearly wasn't over his ex-girlfriend. Instead, the boy I chose had a habit of repeating the same story of his Minnetonka hometown every time I wore my Minnetonka moccasins (which was often). He was subjectively popular and objectively handsome. He had dark hair and dark eyes and a nice smile. He kept watching me. So I let him watch. I let him catch my eye in the dining hall as we waited to refill our coffees, then work to make me smile back. I let him walk me through the snow back to my dorm after a party down the hill, let him talk to me about whatever things he talked about.

For once, the words were not important. What was important was the letting—the letting and the choosing.

I thought I had things figured out. I thought I'd made a smart decision. I thought that being smart would compensate, somehow—for the long-forgotten, ache-sprung fissure; for the way it had begun, of late, to deepen and grow hard. I thought that this was how it went: the script. As in: *I* turn off the lights. *I* say, *Yes*. After, in the morning, *I* say, *No, I don't want to go get breakfast. I'll just see you around.* I thought what mattered was the way I watched him leave: how I waited for the door to fully shut, then gulped cold water, then took out the trash. I thought the thing that mattered was the silk kimono robe I wrapped around my body, and the shower afterwards. How the heat and wet and soap ran over me.

BRUXISMS

I grind my teeth at night. So my dentist tells me. I am thirty. My dentist, one of those ageless slender skin-glow blondes you only find in Southern California. Her smile is fluorescent, the same electric white as her white coat. She makes me feel both old and young at once.

"It might be stress," she suggests. "Perhaps a night guard."

I try to picture such a thing but think instead of orange slices: orbs cut into crescent moons, consumed at soccer games. All us kids, slipping our incisors flush against the quick of dry white pulp. I remember how we'd tuck our upper lips over the rinds, bare citrus smiles, and let the juice explode inside our mouths.

"No thanks," I say. "I'll try to meditate or something; cut back on coffee."

She has an office by the beach. Moonlight Dental, South Coast Highway, Encinitas. Seashell décor, bright yellow walls. Blonde Dentist always wears a dress. Black pumps from Tory Burch and a tasteful string of pearls. Never a hair out of place, and invisible pores. A perfection that unsettles—that suggests I'll never quite shore up the mess of me: a wine stain here, stray eyelash there, one sock forever slumped inside my shoe.

"Get a Sonicare," she says. "They're the best." So, I stop at Target on the drive back home, back up the coast to Los Angeles, back to the apartment my boyfriend—we'll call him A—and I share in Silver Lake and pay $39.95 for a toothbrush labeled "Essence." In the checkout line, I waver, wanting something more. Wine. And maybe lipstick. I pick a color that is bright and bold—a color I would probably describe as very unlike me.

"Revlon Matte Balm," the label reads.
The color: "Standout" [*Remarquable*].

~ ~ ~

Here are my teeth. I am looking in the mirror, homing in. They form a crooked line. A chipped incisor, second from the left. An upper canine, twice as sharp as its mate; the why and how of this unknown. Whole bottom row at slant, bearing west—like full sails in a breeze. When I smile, the composition is a little off: slight gap between my two front teeth, the pink of gums encroaching from beneath the too-high rise of an un-plump upper lip. My teeth are whiter than one might expect—that is, considering the coffee. Lipstick heightens this. Sets them off in tones like "Peony" or "Hope."

At thirty, I don't know, yet, whether this night grinding is something that will get worse or go away. Whether it is stress, or

acid reflux. Whether the damage will be visible or hidden—
unbidden dips and smooth spots only I can feel against my tongue.
All I know is this: you work with what you've got.

~ ~ ~

When I was twenty-three, I spent a winter eating fruit in Baja:
mangoes, apples, oranges, papaya. It was the healthiest I've ever
been—or so it felt. Afterwards, back home in California, I learned
my teeth were full of holes. My hometown dentist, back up in
Northern California, botched the fillings: cheap composite, maybe,
or perhaps the fault of shaking hands. He was getting old. At any
rate, the fillings were not built to last.

By definition, "composite" should be made of recognizable
constituents; the product of at least two factors greater than one.
Composite things may start out fractured, or duplicitous. As in, not
normally found together—but ultimately, capable of joining into
some single entity: compound, alloy, picture. Stronger, possibly,
than each would be alone. Provided that the different factors fit.

Such evidence suggests my fillings would have stayed in better tact
had I asked for gold. At the time, I don't recall my little hometown
dental practice [or, for that matter, my parents] touting this option.
What likely was offered, instead, was a range of other blended
materials—silver amalgam [a medley of copper, silver, mercury,
zinc, and tin], for instance, or an off-white blend of glass and
plastic, or what's vaguely and mysteriously known as *composite
resin*, like the sticky stuff that's tapped from trees. All of these
weaken with time. All of these bear toxic risk. The trick, it seems,

is balance: risk and reward, safety and stability. Of finding a composite you can trust—and even then, still checking every several years to test the infrastructure, to look for rot.

~ ~ ~

Not long after getting those first fillings, I moved south. A moved with me. We'd met in Baja, met and fallen fast in love against the backdrop of that fruit-filled, sun-drenched month. After Mexico, we'd visited each other until he came to stay with me in California, first for a San Francisco summer, then a South Lake Tahoe winter, before we both agreed to settle down in San Diego.

When we moved, I got referrals—doctor, dentist, OBGYN—as one does in a new town, and ended up at Moonlight Dental. The first time we met, Blonde Dentist stuck her tools inside my mouth, then shook her head:

"These fillings are all wrong."

She put a plastic tab against my cheek and flicked a switch. I heard a beep.

"See those lines?" she said. The x-ray image sprung up on the screen: my teeth, close up, less white than I would like and glistening with spit. "Those cracks in the composite? They've got to be replaced."

I nodded.

Not my fault. She made it clear.

Still, I felt this guilt. All that fruit, acid-sweet against my teeth.

Growing up, no one ever told me: how much sugar—acid—rot— might live inside sweet fruit.

~~~

This is how the teeth come in. First there are incisors: four each, on top and bottom, used for biting. Then the primary molars, to chew and grind—called deciduous, like trees, because they shed. Their roots give way for premolars, bicuspids, and grown-up teeth that creep in from the gums. Not until age nine or so do canines come— a set of four, to rip and tear at flesh. Finally, with age, the wisdom teeth, though some pairs fail to sprout.

There is a pattern. A prescription from within—for what to eat, and when, and how to chew. A way in which my body will expect— that is, permit—me to be hungry. My teeth assert control. Their shape, their fitness—solid first, then filled with holes, then ground. Gum recession might someday change the way I chew. A rotted filling leaves the cavity, the price for too much sweetness, gaping open. The pain each time I bite down hard [raw broccoli florets, burnt toast], a warning: *shore up this mess.*

~ ~ ~

I get home from the dentist in a funk. It's Friday night. I pull into the driveway, wishing I had plans. A and I live just off Sunset Boulevard. Despite the prime location, we don't go out that often. He doesn't like the noise, the press, of crowds. We stay in a lot. Mostly, I don't mind this. I've taken a domestic turn, taken to cooking nice dinners, plating salads, adding garnish. Mostly, I'm content.

But right now, it's Friday night, and I'm in Los Angeles, and I'm craving lights and stranger's faces. I think about Blonde Dentist and her pretty dresses, my new lipstick, and feel the urge to tidy up; look "put together," as my mom might say. I check the mail, climb the stairs. Maybe we could get dressed up, walk together to the quiet French bar down the street—the one with all the darkened wood and oil paintings on the walls, strong drinks, big ice cubes, Moroccan pillows strewn across the giant leather couch.

Except that when I turn the key and walk inside, A isn't home.

So I tear the foil off the bottle of Target shiraz, then the plastic wrapper from my tube of Revlon Matte Balm lipstick. Pour a glass of wine. Stand alone in front of the bathroom mirror and smooth on "Standout:" first along the border of my lips, then filling in the plumper parts.

Press both pads of flesh together. Dab with tissue. Bare my teeth.

The color looks good: flame and cherry, dark and rich against my pale white skin. Not *remarquable*, perhaps, but close. Still, I won't go out. Not like this, alone, and with my lips all red and loud, my teeth, by contrast, whiter than I've earned. These teeth belong to someone else—someone brazen and seductive that A doesn't know, that even I don't know particularly well. Someone who intrigues and frightens me. I don't think I trust her. She will stay inside with me, and drink Shiraz, and maybe move and sway around the coffee table in the dark, her arms outstretched. Our fingers barely touching.

~~~

The medical term for "grinding teeth" is bruxism. Bruxism might be caused by stress, anxiety, anger, tension, rage. Or there's hyperactive personality, or acid reflux, or malocclusion, or psychiatric backlash. There's the simple need to cope, and force of habit. There's alcohol and coffee, sleep apnea and snoring and fatigue.

In other words, the root cause of bruxism has nothing to do with teeth. It's borne of minds in motion; nocturnal churn of language hitting bone. In other words, the brain—the jaw—revolts at night. Fights, perhaps, against prescription. Rules for how to hunger; how to chew. As for me, I never know if I've been grinding. I only know those nights A wakes me: tells me he can feel my jawbone working hot against his shoulder as we sleep.

DARK STORAGE

"…I had some idea that the gold light would make me feel better, but I did not bother to weight the curtains correctly and all that summer the long panels of transparent golden silk would blow out the windows and get tangled…"

~Joan Didion, "Goodbye to All That"

GREEN

Sometimes it is easier to see the ends of things, and harder to see how they began. If one particular thing—a relationship, for instance, or a season—has just ended. Has ended so recently that time is still inching into melt-drip spring. Sometimes, there's a sudden change in light. Language, too, begins to drip. The sudden yellow-orange sunlight startles with its marmalade-tinted brightness. Words take on the honeyed echo of a voiceover. What I mean is, sometimes the end of something isn't so much clear as it is a kind of immersion: where you, too, succumb to spring—permit your neck nerves to relax and melt beneath the syrupy weight of flame-flecked marmalade. All around you, there is light that catches you and clings, as if your skin were the gossamer wings of a fly.

Take me, for instance. For months, the nerves inside my neck have been constricted. For months, I've felt the weight of this: veined arms, dark hair, a heavy love. The weight of eight full years, and how we met—[his hands and lips, salt waves, dry Baja palms]—and how, for me, that memory has since lightened, thinned. Blurred with distance like a film dissolve.

But now, because of this ending, the tension gives way. Now I almost feel like I'm inside the light. Sometimes, I feel like giving in. My body wants to uncoil. My lips catch hints of sweetness. And because I'm talking about myself—that is, telling you my version of this season, ending, sweet—the sweetness might be something in particular. Say, the sweetness of North Idaho in spring: tulips and exploding crocuses, gold-green-soaked Palouse prairie, hills that roll and roll and green so green it melts right through the atmosphere.

It is a porous green. It turns me porous. Lands against my tongue and tastes like marmalade, like citrus, and the smell of good light in the morning.

OFF RAMP
Sometimes the end of something is a kind of unraveling. Sometimes, the thing that ends is not so much a thing as it is a place.

Say, a city. Say, Los Angeles.

OPTICS
Except of course I know that green—or any other color [yellow-gold, sky-blue, blade of grass]—probably can't land upon my tongue. Because it is nothing more than sheen: the surface of an object that my optic nerve perceives and then perverts. Reflection

or absorption, or a little bit of both. A version of a version of a thing.

BROWN

It is easy for me to see how Los Angeles ended, and harder for me to see how it began. Not because I don't remember, but because the beginnings were so many. Because they blur and overlap. Because, for me, Los Angeles began inside my bones. When I first saw Los Angeles, I would have been about three years old. It would have been summertime. I would have seen it from the backseat of my parents' boxy Volvo 240 sedan as we flew along the I-5 South—past San Jose, Los Banos, Buttonwillow, Gorman; past Castaic and The Grapevine, then Valencia, then Burbank, then sputtering, at last, down to a crawl [as one does, eventually, from any direction, when arriving in Los Angeles] and merging with the sludge of cars and smog and asphalt heat in a collective westward push onto the 101.

We would have pushed between the high-rise towers of Downtown and on to Central, to the house with the hot tub filled with plastic floating vegetables where my mother's best friend [who'd married my father's best friend] lived with many cats and dogs and records and most likely marijuana plants, though I didn't know about that then. We would have been headed to Disneyland. But that year, and every year thereafter, we would first have made our way into the city. We would have driven through Hollywood, and I would have gaped at the palm trees, the brownness, the occasional Rolls or Bentley, the Capitol Records building, the storied turrets of the Chateau Marmont.

Could I have rolled the window down myself? Been old enough, arms long enough, to reach the plastic lever on the right-hand passenger door? Felt the brownness of the hot dry wind against my palms?

MERGE

Sometimes the thing that ends is not so much a thing or even a place as it is a feeling. Perhaps that feeling is love. Or it is dreaming. Or it is a kind of rupture—of memory, connection. Sometimes, perhaps it is a tangle of all three: a golden plait torn ragged by the winds of spring and waves of porous green.

OCCIPITAL

The brain processes visions through the retina, transferring data first via the thalamus onto a whisper-wall of tissue called the visual cortex. It is bigger than the plastic cap of a film canister, smaller than a camera lens cover. It hovers somewhere near the back of the brain, floating in the occipital lobe. It waits to see the surface of things—floorboards, jam jars, cacti needles—bent against the light.

GOLD

Let's suppose I had to choose. Let's suppose I had to lay a finger down—select a single, fated, switchflick moment—when what I'm calling "Los Angeles" began. What moment did I feel the city's heat-bleached streets—blue on gold on black in every season—reaching up to stroke my skin?

When I first saw Los Angeles like this, I was twenty-seven, and it was just past New Year's Day, and A and I were getting on an E175 regional jet at Bob Hope Burbank Airport to fly back to San Diego. I wore a brand-new cream-white patterned blouse from Anthropologie that was very beautiful and had cost far too much; that still held within its inexplicably soft weave some of the gold and rarity and unseasonable warmth of the city. Because, of course, the January air outside *was* warm [as, when in Los Angeles, it always seems to be]. And something of that warmth stayed with me: as I sat against my pleather seat and breathed recycled air; as I leaned against A's tanned and sturdy arm and watched the Burbank backlots shrink and morph and glitter in the distance, as in intro clips for Warner Brothers films. As I realized [in the same thoughtbreath in which A said *imagine if we moved here*], I'd been imagining it, too.

Back then, we were still trying. Back then, something about sitting on an airplane on a January evening, just past New Year's, looking out the window at Los Angeles, soothed the vague and sprawling notion of *the future* into something warmsoft; something welcome. And as I settled back into a pool of plastic-window-filtered sun, some instinct—programmed by Warner Brothers and Turner Classic Movies, by Disneyland and coastal drives and palm tree curves and sunshine bright on swimming pools, by shadows falling black against the Bernadino Mountain peaks and by the warmth, that warmth again of sinking to my boyfriend's shoulder as we craned our necks to watch the last of golden-brownness fade— informed me that Los Angeles, or at least my feeling of it, would never be quite the same again.

But perhaps you already know that. Perhaps you can tell where this is going.

SURFACE STREETS/ECHO PARK

Of course, it might have been some other city [had circumstance been different and the time been different and had I been different]. It might have been Dublin or New York or San Francisco—and it very nearly was. But because I am talking about myself, and because I am talking about the truth and not what might have been [and yet, because of what was true, I have no choice but to include what might have been], I am talking about Los Angeles.

Los Angeles: a city that has always held a rigid sway over my body, asserted a magnetic pull over my blood. A power buried under palms and sand and grit, or maybe shed from city lights spilled into darkness that unfolds each night just like a reel of film. Its power drew me in. Drew me, somehow, down the same small maze of side streets off Sunset—Fountain, Effie, Sanborn Bates—where my mother had once lived, some forty years before I'd ever even heard of Silver Lake or Echo Park. Where she had lived against the hills, in the shadow of those rising palms, in the shadow of the Downtown high-rise towers, in a basement apartment beset with floods and cockroaches.

And yet, because she [I?] had been in love, a place of happiness.
No, not quite a place; a feeling.
Sometimes, I confess, I have confused the two.

Los Angeles was where she had lived with Steve, the man who might [had circumstances been different and the time been different and my mother been different] have been my father: long red braided hair, green and white checked pants in all the pictures, bachelor's degree in film. A carpenter who once got paid in Pringles for fitting fire doors into the flophouses Downtown. Steve, who called my mother his "Spicy Ravioli," and drove a motorcycle, and took her to see Charlie Chaplin marathons at the Los Feliz Village Cinema; the same small theater where, forty-three years later, I would go with A, my own long-haired, motorcycle-riding, photograph-taking, aspiring actor boyfriend, and drink beers on sunny summer afternoons and sit in back and lean against his arm and feel his warmth and think *yes, this could be happiness.*

SUBTRACTION

Spend enough time in Los Angeles, and you may find that film and vision start to bleed together. Start to infiltrate your sense of color, distance, shape. Take me, for instance. Here is what I've come to know: about color, and how it pertains to reels of film—of Kodak's Kodachrome, to be precise. Kodak introduced Kodachrome in 1913. It was the first film of its kind to use what's known as subtractive color. Previous iterations [Autochrome, Dufaycolo] had always employed the so-called additive color method—that is, the use of discrete color elements that only became visible upon acute inspection. But Kodachrome employed just two color pairs: blue-green and red-orange. The resultant film, reintroduced in 1935, came to be known as non-substantive; color-reverse, and is still appreciated by contemporary archivists—both for this reverse approach to image rendering, and for its unique dark-storage longevity.

BROWN

When I was twenty-one, I spent a week in Spain. My friend V and I traveled, perpetually cava-drunk and giddy, west from Barcelona to Madrid, then squirreled east again until Valencia. We were headed, ultimately, to the beach. It was early summer, June, and looking out the windows on that train trip to the coast was like traveling in time, like sitting in the Volvo on the I-5 South: same feel of El Camino, same view of sunbaked brownness. Uncanny. As if a piece of me, despite my pink-pale skin and scant Spanish, was somehow, by virtue of the mirrored land, the echoes in the feeling of the air, rooted here. Was somehow of this place or knew it well. Just like the way my child's palm knew hot dry wind was code for *Angel City: we are almost there.*

SURFACE STREETS/SUNSET JUNCTION

In retrospect, it seems to me that those days before I knew the names of all the streets off Sunset were happier than the ones that came later. But perhaps you already know that. Perhaps you can tell where this is going.

Part of what I want to tell you is what it's like to realize you are no longer all that young in Los Angeles. How all those old stories and glimpses from windows and afternoons of beer and sun and warmth eventually add up, and how the city's golden sheen deceives—then melts away. For that is how those two short years seem to me now: like a slowed-down sequence, artfully arranged. Rose-tinged dissolves. Old-fashioned trick shots. Two short years slowed down and stalled and spreading out. Prettily unraveling the six long years that came before. Clever angles rendering our brief stint in Silver Lake—the sweaty walks around Echo Park Lake in summer, the nights I'd pan-fry fish from the Farmer's Market, and we'd eat together on the balcony, the empty Soju bottles hidden underneath the sink—into something mistakable for happiness. Rendering the two of us, A and me, into rose-tinted lovers sitting side-by-side and laughing, always laughing [even when we were, in fact, quite silent, stirring drinks with elegant steel toothpicks, reading menus we had read before], our fingers intertwined beneath the bougainvillea, our credit card bills swelling month to month, our hearts still trying to convince us that somewhere, just around the corner, there would come a greengold paycheck.

Something about the heat and light and color of Los Angeles managed to subtract from this—our shared equation—all the nights where no amount of talking, silence, holding, wanting, could make it better. Subtraction, non-substantive—color working in reverse. Such nights nearly always ended with me crying in the shower while he sat, staring off into the blinking red and yellow lights of El Pollo Loco through the shadowy bamboo and palm, combing fingers through the tangle of his long black hair, leaving little nests like snakes against the rust-brown terra cotta that I'd find and sweep and sweep into the bin each palm-bright morning. Nests left so often that the birds moved in.

PALINOPSIA

Once an image makes it to the occipital lobe, where is it stored? In the dark, or in the light, and for how long? Consider: dark-storage longevity. Consider: canisters of Kodak film. Consider: time. What is the difference? Between perceiving—tasting—*knowing*—a color, then recalling or retrieving it again? What is the difference between the flick of an eyelash up against the yellow gold of springtime light, and the passing of one year, or eight, or thirty-one?

Visual memory, much like vision of color itself, is always working at a disadvantage: composing a version of a version of a thing that only ever just resembles or reflects a color [green], an object [tanned and sturdy arm]. Sometimes, visual memory is disrupted even further. Sometimes, the brain produces a persistent repetition of the same image [heat-bleached streets; gold-soaked-hardwood-floors] over and over and over again—even after the stimulus has been removed. Even after the whole perception of the thing is in the past.

This dysfunction is known as *palinopsia*.
This dysfunction is known as *memory*.

GOLD

For all its storied excesses, Los Angeles was surprisingly affordable. At least in terms of rent, that is. Of course I knew that it would cost me something else, sooner or later—even if some part of me belonged there, came from there—but when I first arrived, as I have said, I was twenty-seven, and everything was golden, and A and I were still trying, and I figured that I knew myself, and that I'd be able, in the end, to pay whatever it would cost. Besides, Los Angeles has a way of making one believe in possibilities again: even one like me, at twenty-seven, with no interest in "the industry," no taste for spray-on tans. Los Angeles has a way of making sure that all things fade with softness. A way of throwing on a newborn blue each morning as I drove down Sunset Boulevard.

In Los Angeles, for a little while, nothing was irrevocable; everything was within reach. The way that golden film caressed my skin. The way it coated everything—cream-white curtains, thrift-store couch, hardwood floors and Bulleit bourbon and the veins along A's forearms that one night we drank too much and talked about a wedding and how charmed we were by the idea of succulents in Mason jars for centerpieces, by that little inn in Ojai for the reception, by sunsets in the desert. The golden flicker of the screen as I scrolled through images of crocheted dresses on Pinterest, as A sketched the outline of a custom ring on notebook paper from the hotel where we'd tied each other up and fucked one night in Dallas.

SURFACE STREETS/SILVER LAKE BOULEVARD

Was it coincidence that we landed there, in Silver Lake, near Echo Park—my mother's own tangle of lost haunts? When we first decided on the move, A and I sat down with a bunch of maps and Craigslist. We called all our friends who'd ever lived there, asked around and scoped out neighborhoods and drew up price comparisons and crime comparisons and sought out farmer's markets, walkability stats, proximity to bus lines, parking, and happy hours. We toyed with moving, first, to Highland Park, then Korea Town, then Culver City, Venice, Pico, Mid City, Palms.

One afternoon, A drove from San Diego up to Silver Lake to take an improv workshop and got lost. He never made it to the workshop. Instead, he stopped at the intersection of Silver Lake and Sunset Boulevard, and got out, and bought a café con leche at Café Tropical, and took a walk around the neighborhood, and picked up some alt weekly magazines, and bought a piece of sweetbread. After that, we both went back together, and of course we knew— that this was it. The place for us. Or at least it was for a little while.

Was it coincidence that brought us there? Or fate? Or some peculiar inheritance? Or perhaps a tangle of all three: whispers of my mother's life infiltrating mine, our shared missteps, our loves—

these threads of brown and gold perpetually drawn to one another, even as I pick-pull them apart?

PALETTE

Steve McCurry, the photojournalist responsible for the still-iconic "Afghan Girl" portrait made famous on the cover of *National Geographic Magazine* back in 1984, had this to say about his love of Kodachrome in an interview for *Vanity Fair*: "If you have good light and you're at a fairly high shutter speed, it's going to be a brilliant color photograph. It had a great color palette. It wasn't too garish…Kodachrome had more poetry in it, a softness, an elegance…you take it out of the box and the pictures are already brilliant."

What I mean is this: sometimes, all that matters is good light.

MERGE

I was in a curious position in Los Angeles. It never occurred to me, at least during those early days, that I was not living a real life there. In my imagination this was it, and we would stay, and we would keep on trying. In my dreams, there would come a someday when that green-golden-money wave would wash over us both; a someday when that whiskey-soaked, golden-coated night of imagined desert sunsets and jarred succulents would come to fruition.

But I was not so very young in Los Angeles, and neither was A. And at some point, it became clear that the golden rhythm we'd been hoping for was not just broken, but in fact had never quite begun.

ACCURACY

Visual memory is not always accurate. This is hardly a surprise. How could it be, when each vision is a surface, is a flavor, is a bending—an interpretation? How could it be, when each vision can easily be further misled by external conditions or events? Studies have shown that those exposed to misleading information [e.g. *it is always summertime*; e.g. *the sky is always blue, and all the gold is real*, e.g. *we were still trying*, e.g. *the hills are green, and therefore wholly different from the gold*] are less able to recall the real visual details of the said event. Whether this misinformation was provided before or after the event in question does not matter.

GREEN

ne·on /*nēän*/(noun).

The ancient Greek for which is *neos*—something new.

OFF RAMP

The last time I was in Los Angeles was in a warm and gentle April. I was thirty-one years old, and back in town for a writing conference, and everyone was giddy and eager to bare their legs and put on skirts and sit outside at café bars and drink spring drinks with things like gin and spritz and lemon. Many of the people I knew were digging in their heels, and staying put, and getting jobs on TV shows or teaching improv workshops.

As for me, I had already left. Just temporarily, of course—or that is what I'd thought, at least, the day I signed the papers for a three-year graduate program in Idaho. But perhaps you already know that. Perhaps you can tell where this is going.

The last time I was in Los Angeles, it was warm and blue and gold and brown. I stayed four days. I slept next to A in the Silver Lake apartment, my head on his shoulder, my hands kept to myself. We didn't kiss. We held each other over and over. I spent my days catching Uber and Lyft cars up and down beneath the bluest sky on Sunset Boulevard, shaking hands with writers and editors and magazine people and eating exorbitantly overpriced bags of potato chips and apples in the window-filtered-sunlight of the Downtown convention center. I spent my last night in Los Angeles with A at Jay's Bar, the two of us toasting to our agreed-upon separateness—"at least for now"—and all we might explore.

I was thirty-one years old. I stayed four days, and then I packed my things and took a morning flight back to Idaho, back to the northwest of the northeast. What I mean is this: that somehow, moving backwards from the coast into this green, this green—it felt like moving forwards; like propulsion; perhaps even a bit like happiness.

Before I left, I'd hugged A goodbye on the concrete steps, setting down the spare duffle bag I'd brought along to fill with books and high-heeled, ankle-strap suede shoes; with gym pants and my favorite Fiestaware pink mug. I remember that we'd held each other, and that the sun had already turned from soft to hot, and that I'd pressed my cheek against the tightness of his jaw. I remember knowing, then, that our apartment was becoming his apartment; that the golden film along the hardwood floors and thrift store couch and bourbon whiskey bottles and succulents left dying on the patio had been absorbed—replaced by morning light, by the bend and scent of springtime neon green. I remember blooms of lavender against the sidewalk, and the gray-green of their stems. I remember noticing a lizard: how he sunned his dry brown body near the purple-painted gate.

II.

THAT SAME SUMMER

I.

Trace the outline of these fields: alfalfa, lentil, wheat. Green like citrus. Green like lasers. Arm stretched out as far as it will stretch beyond the window of his Ford Escape.

Your fingers graze the line of the horizon, where blueness yields into Palouse. Your fingers trace the line along his forearm, etched in dark green ink: a line that ebbs and rolls just like these hills he loves—that you begin to think you might love, too. A horizon line above which rises one clean circle, full-moon round: circumference measuring the same size loop your thumb and index finger purchase when they touch.

> *It's hard to deny that everything's connected.*
> > This is how he phrases it—the circle, what it means.
> > You nod your head.
> > > You ask yourself: *Are we?*

Because this sweetness is so new. Beset by qualifiers [as in, *nothing serious*, as in, *no commitments*]. And yet it *is* sweet. Sweet the way hot lemon water slides like honey down your throat the third time you wake up with him, with B, and realize he bought lemons just for you. Sweet the way a bad recording of his voice and un-tuned banjo swells— [bashfulness a shiver up your neck, phone gone hot against your ear]—at Reagan, as you're waiting for a plane:

Come back home to Idaho.
       Or maybe that is not the title of the song.
       After all, it is a made-up song.
       After all, these lines are all made up—equations,
       rules—between you.

Until this spring, you haven't slept alone in years. Eight, to be exact—eight springs, eight summers, thirty-two long seasons— spent with someone else beside you, always.

      [What this means: now solitude is sweet.
        That is, if you miss that someone else
         sometimes, you do not miss his body:
          in your bed, or out of it;
          in your car, or mouth,
          or kitchen]

But now, so quickly, it is summer.
Now, so quickly after A, there's B: *his* bed, *his* body—
lined and circled. And sometimes, when you wake up on your sliver of his full-sized mattress, both of you pressed east towards the edge because his cat has joined you [and his cat takes precedence], you think: this is not—

—that is, this is bitter;

[as in, *nightbreath*; as in, *isn't what you want*]

Until you wake again at dawn. Until you turn to find he's poured a tiny, warm, and humming blue-gray lump of cat between your bodies. Until he draws you close against his chest and slips his left arm—that lined and scored and circled arm—around your shoulders. You study it again. You wait for him to rest the bristle of his mustache near the big vein at your temple.

April. May. June. July—

June.

He goes back to Kansas for vacation. He leaves you keys—even though you've only been together for two months; even though *together* is a funny thing to call two people who are definitely separate [and really, you're not sure what *together* even means—for people, bodies—anymore]. All he asks is that you feed the cat. Sleep with her a night or two, perhaps.

[This is how you know: like waking up
with sudden fingers on the verge
of going numb—]

You hesitate. You worry expectations. But his place is right above the bar. Easy and convenient. And you really do adore the cat. One night, after drinking two shots of Fernet [because you tried to hang out with his friends, but found yourself increasingly uncomfortable, uncertain, and you do not even like Fernet—] you skip the walk uphill to your apartment, and instead walk back to his.

For the first time: alone.

You peel off your jeans. You slip on a pair of his striped boxer briefs. You stand barefoot in his brown and cream and yellow kitchen, scooping spoonful after drunken spoonful of Jiff peanut butter from the jar.

> To be fair: you do this at home sometimes, as well. At home, you often feel ashamed. But somehow—in his kitchen, in his underwear, eating his cheap non-organic peanut butter—you are unabashed. Brazen, even. Intimate—

> > [with this: Trojan Horse of
> > might-be love, wheeled and parked
> > between your hips—]

You brush your teeth. You sit on the toilet. The cat scratches her litter, and you talk to her: about this night, about Fernet—about the bitter taste that lingers, and the weather. You try to hold her after, but she runs away.

Then you fall asleep in white and green and bamboo-printed sheets: Arm & Hammer clean, and only just familiar. Remnant cat hairs on the pillow as you drift.

You wake at five AM to some strange pressure at your chest, and warmth, and a vibration. The cat is kneading at your shoulder: keeping time. One gray paw and then the other, back and forth, her purring audible above the din of dump trucks.

For the first time: just you and she, alone.

All morning long, she climbs and clambers on your body: sniffs your cheek, or licks your palm, or burrows at your breast. And though you tell him all about it afterward—and though the two of you will laugh—you never tell him this:

> [Her pink sandpaper tongue, sweet-scratching at your skin, is intimate—but also something more. Like love, perhaps. Or cheating. Something so close to possession—the having of it, or the losing]

II.

That same summer, you turned wanton. Ate until you spilled. Drank until you felt the pinch of denim and elastic—belt-dig at your waist. Not visibly. Not in a way that others would have noticed. Just enough to feel more comfortable naked than in clothes: without stricture, unrestrained, your softly curving flesh made free against the air.

Even now, tonight—this one-year-later-May, this new near-summer-dusk—your friend J [as she is pinning up her hair, testing her curling iron, bare face stripped and spotted, shining before makeup], even now, she tells you: *but you're tall; you carried it so well; no one would have known.*

Still: *you* knew; you *still* know.

Sometimes, that is what's important. How you felt the signs—

[what this means: *this isn't what you want*]

—then numbed yourself with apricots and buttered toast, kisses and good gin. You know how your body opened up, then filled—brimming with the excess of infatuation.

[The way you felt: like satin stuffed with stones.
Like tires, or the spilling of a melted candle
pooled around a jam jar,
pooled around the bottom of some vessel much too small
for all its waxing—hot and wet, and sticking afterward]

The memory of something burned, then held.

Held, but not *produced*. This is important. Not a filling up with some *new* thing—motherly and ample. Not a making, but a gripping: nervous, frightened even, body layering itself over and over in defense—

That same summer, you stayed hungry. Everything you did, you did because you knew that time was passing like a flybuzz, like a Vespa. Like the budding sprigs of lavender, ringed and held against the sidewalk where you park your car: plump-wet-purple for an instant, wind-dry-flaking within days.

This is how it goes: a summer, or a sideways love. Your body knew this. It still knows. Your favorite things became the pricking bees of sweetness: Vouvray wine uncorked too soon—wine that wouldn't last the weekend. Olive oil cake and peaches. Rainer cherries— smooth round, tight-skinned—in the fridge.

Still: you forget more slowly than these sweet things die. You grow older. You have many things to think about. You find yourself, at times, so sick of learning. So eager to lie back and stick just like a fly in honey. Dead and slow, and nothing to be done.

But that same summer, you could not see any of this. Not exactly. That is, you saw it all the time—but never in the cherries or the olive oil cake, or at the bottom of a wine glass where the sediment sank low. You saw it only when you also felt or saw your swelling, sweating body—in the shower, in the mirror—

—caught its edges.

[A sun-crown halo during an eclipse]

[Something that could send you blind]

Now, tonight, it is a different summer.

Now, you start to notice—understand—

[What that summer filling-up was telling you:]

Now you sit here, peering into J's bathroom. Stool-perched in the narrow hall of her apartment. It is a different summer. You've since traded Vouvray for Vermentino, dry white wine with just a hint of fizz. Spartan in its stringency against your tongue, its tartness down your throat. Now you watch her as she dusts her skin—still winter-pale—with powder, then with blush.

She is going on a date. Someone new. Some stranger who just walked into the bar—such a rarity in this small town.

Now it is one-year-later-May.
Now it is near-summer-dusk.

[Watch the dry wax break
beneath my index fingernail]

III.

That same summer ended.
That same summer, in so many ways, is back again.
That same summer *is.*

[as in, it *should* have ended; as in, *it repeats*]

How could you have known?
    Or: perhaps you did.

                [here, you check yourself]
            [you know more than you let on—]
           [beneath a tooth; inside your hips—]

This is summer in a too-small town.
This is summer in the land of rivers, not the land of waves.
This is then and now:

           [That is: this is that same summer, *turned*]

Slowly, you are learning. You learn that rivers loop. A river curls in
on itself. This is how it goes: the way of land-bound water, or two
summers in the same place in a row.

Now, again, so quickly: summer.
Now, instead, so quickly: your turn to want, to count the days—

        [Peel a word like *anniversary* from the label
        on this same Grüner Veltliner—the first
        you drank together—from the soft flesh
        just behind your jawbone, or along your
        lower lip—]

There is gravel in your throat. The cottonwoods. The brightness of late May. Silence sits uneasy with you: sticks to the untidy edges of *over* and *again*.

Between these two: a false distinction.
Clever like a stretch of fishing line.
[as in, *gasp for air;* as in, *isn't what you want(ed) in the first place, anyway*]
April. May. June. July—
June.

The moon is quick-teeth-waning. Your eyes and nose are full of pollen. There is mud inside your body—red like dirty clay, not fully sprung into the kind of red that counts—and it wants out. Like this summer, your filling up, your wantonness, has turned. This is summer at a slant. You are getting skinny. S keeps telling you the same thing that she tells her angsting teenage daughter: *go get yourself a full-fat latte.*

[Yesterday, you accidentally bit
down on the right side of your tongue.
You figured this was how the universe
might say, *stop talking.*
So you did.
You stopped]

Last week, you and S sat out on the fancy restaurant patio, on Main Street, drinking crisp rosé. Last week, he rode by you on his bicycle. Cut-off sleeves, sun-red skin, lined and circled arms.

Rode by not thirty seconds after you'd mentioned that it had been at least a month since you'd crossed paths with him—this, despite the fact that you now live in the same building. That the odds were stacked. That it was probably high time.

He then rode by not once, but twice.
You said *again*—

[as in, *nearly*]

This is summer. You begin to see the pattern.
You have so many questions. Such as: when does coincidence become logic? When does logic become clairvoyance?

[What you mean to say is this:
what's true is neither *over* nor *again*.
It is both. It is porous: lightened
by the late-May sun, and twisting—
—it is full of holes]

Tomorrow, your friend C will walk side-by-side with you from campus to downtown.

He will say *I love the summers here.*

You will say, *Me too, but not right now.*

C: *What do you mean by that?*

You: *Doesn't sunshine sometimes feel like an assault?*

> You will think he doesn't understand. You will grow impatient. You will think he doesn't see what you are asking him to see. About this, you will be both right and wrong. You won't know the difference for a while yet— that is, not until the summer closes in; not until the cottonwoods swarm down beneath the awning of the coffee shop. Swarm and grope your nostrils and your teeth.

In the meantime, you look out. See the loop and patchwork of Palouse. You look up. See the floating cotton: shadows like cell clusters, lakes, or tiny storms. You look in the mirror. See your body like a window square. See the windows of your apartment—yours, then B's. Windows lined along the same brick wall, looking out along the same side of the street.

Count the squares between.

> [Peel and peel.
> Remind yourself:
> *this isn't what you want*]

Peer through your window: see him walking, framed against the glass.

> [He will keep on walking past]
> [He will stay within the frame]

ON SHAME

You do not ride a bike.

People misunderstand this. They say: *you could get a used one cheap.*

What's true is that you do not ride or own—or want to ride or want to own—a bike. You do not like to move so fast, so high up off the ground: your feet locked up in pedals, your fingers clasping bars. What's true is that you've never liked this kind of speed. Hard plastic stuck between your legs.

It isn't that you haven't tried it. It's that you have—and every time you ride you fall and scrape your knee and break the skin or bend an elbow.

Eventually, you choose to break the pattern.

[Some choices are easier than others]

You found the Have-A-Tampa cigar box at an antique store downtown. The box is heavy cardboard: cream and tangerine. A pretty woman in a red skirt rests both brown hands on her hips.

The box tucks neatly in between the books beside your bed, a dozen or so, slipped into a sideways-flipped French wine case. Inside the box: four Lifestyles non-latex condoms, one matte black vibrator, one small jar of Vicks Vapo Rub. The latter items you use often: either at night [the rub] or in the morning [the vibrator].

You hide the Vicks jar in the bathroom on those nights when you don't sleep alone.

When is hunger ever without hints of shame?

     [How to reconcile—

     that every time, you cried and skidded off the path into the pussy willow;

     that every time, if only for an instant, speed and being so high up was also fun?]

shame

SHām/

<u>noun</u>:

     1. a painful feeling of humiliation or distress caused by the consciousness of wrong or foolish behavior.

        1.1 a loss of respect or esteem; dishonor.

1.2 [count noun] a person, action, or situation that brings a loss of respect or honor.

2. [*in singular*] a regrettable or unfortunate situation or action.

<u>verb:</u>

1.2 cause (someone) to feel inadequate by outdoing or surpassing them.

The first time you have anal sex, you don't. Not really.

[What this means:]

You are hungover, and B is hungover. Also, B may or may not even *be* your boyfriend—as in, you have been dating for seven months, but only call each other *daters*, which is cute but only for so long—and so he is pressed up against your back, and both of you still smell of mezcal, cardamom and lemon, last night's fancy drinks and dance floor sweat, and he is pressing against your ass and you are pressing back but on your period so instead of slipping him inside you let him slide between the fat flesh folds because you're turned on now and everything is slippery and it's a nice sensation in its way—smooth and superficial—and besides, he loves this sliding, he is breathing heavy on your neck, he is whispering more tenderly than usual into the smoke and mezcal tangle of your hair and asking *are you sure this is okay?*

This is when you realize that he thinks he is inside of you.

This is when you realize that it is November; that you've been having sex since May. That he is your boyfriend whether you like it or not. That he does not know the difference.

You let him think and think and slide and know this way until he comes.

Aging is an inconvenience.

[What this means: you are getting bad at self-delusion]

Your studio apartment is a box. White paint and honey wood. Later, in the spring, after the two of you break up, you will live inside. Sometimes you will stand at the window, both hands on your hips. There is a red dress that you love—yellow flowers, red pearl buttons. It is bright, more coral than red, and when you wear it, people notice you. There is a blooming yellow tree strung up with white-blink lights outside the double windows. Big square windows. Wires tangle in the branches when it storms.

shame
SHām/
<u>noun:</u>

1. a photograph on Instagram: eight bicycles—bright colors—propped along the sky-blue-painted wall outside the bar. A caption: *pub crawl on bikes; perfect Sunday afternoon.*

>1.1. even when you first met, when he was still infatuated: you would never, could never, be perfect—that is, surpass—

>1.2. a recollection; knowing—

verb:

2. never to give head to anyone you do not trust; lip-bite anxious; fear of what might get inside.

>2.1. to drip or spill; that is, to demonstrate excess—

>2.2. to offer him, instead: your cheek; the white square of your back; deep pillow lines against—

The second time you have anal sex is, in fact, the first.

[What this means:]

Once again, you are on your period. Once again, his body is pressed up against you, sideways, slipping back and forth. Except this time: no confusion. Except this time: push—gasp—shove—all the way inside—and you can't catch your breath against it. Hunger. Sudden, breath-sweat, hair stuck to your neck despite the snow outside, and so you press—against—him:

[that is, all your unknown empty
wanting to be filled]

[How to reconcile—
is the instinct to bite down against the drypink of your lips the same
as wanting him to press you back?]

Your memory, even when it fails you, is relentless.

No definition does it justice. The gutting that you feel when, four
months after he first fucks you in the ass, he says *I want to be free.*
You suck for air against the knife-turn: belly, chest. Not because it
isn't over—as in, you and him—but because of how you opened.
Because of how you let yourself be hungry. Because of how you let
him tease and play and prick and press and shove himself inside:

[a contract]

That is: you once felt freedom to be unapologetic in your appetites.
Even if you hated how you felt afterwards—in the morning, in the
bathroom, your pelvic bowl flipped upside-down and addled in its
gravity, thick and slow for days—you also craved the choice to
say—

—craved
—your own capitulation:

to his hunger: for you: his wanting of your strange, most hidden depths. Because, to you, this meant something like trust. Hunger for your own voice saying *yes* and *yes* and *more* and *just a little deeper* and

[craved]

You have been ashamed:
    of bicycles and bitten lips
    of fear
    of speed
    of being unchosen

The smart of asphalt on your knee, or chewed flesh washed over with lemon juice or vinegar. The sight of his quick neck outside the box of your apartment, the box in which you live—his body moving past your window, torso walking through the square, the blue ridge of his Royals cap rounding the corner, all the cells inside you knowing—

[What this means: that even in a red dress on a storm-dark night—gone images and smells clicking and dripping past your eyes and down your throat, the rain a metronome, the tangled lights like music notes, trapped amongst the leaves—]

—your want is hollow; your love, perhaps,
was not—that is, was never.
Eventually, you must choose to break the pattern.

[Some choices are easier than others]

Now it is spring. Now the nights you most wish to forget are nights
when you imagine that the fact of six or seven gin & sodas might
invert the fact of loneliness. These are the nights where you will try
to make your waving eyes inside their sockets focus on a stranger or
a friend or anyone whose eyes rest long enough on yours, whose
hands rest long enough upon your knee, for you to drink more gin
and see if it will silence all the stronger parts of you that only want
to sleep and wake up sober and alone. Want to wake up smelling
clean instead of sticky like the bar and cigarettes and toothbrushless
and dry-mouth-sick beside a body that you do not love.

To know one's self a little better with each passing year—
that is, to know one's self as such—hollow and particular—

[an inconvenience]

Then again, you fully comprehend the silliness of trying to make sense:

      —as body
      —as anything at all

Take this afternoon, right now, as an example: you, stuck in the middle airplane seat in some gigantic, metal sky-tube, eating too-sweet peanuts, drinking too-sweet Coke [which normally you hate, except the bubbles calm you down sometimes when it is hot and you are stuck up in the sky], your elbows too big not to bump both of your neighbors, your insides stuffed with air and pinching like an empty plastic water bottle. As such: this is you. And you experience unspecialness like nausea—like muggy weather at the beach. It makes you sweat just slightly, a light film of fear and wetness underneath your breasts and down your neck. You notice the redundancy of all your pinks and browns and bones and blood and lips and teeth—notice it the way you notice dry eyes and a sneaking body odor, seeping out against the weak defense of spray-on lavender deodorant.

You observe the pointlessness of draping all this stuff—your body—washing it and spraying it with lavender deodorant and donning coral-red-dress-cotton just to keep from dripping—

      —being honest
      —spilling over

Still: you've aged some, lately. Thirty-two is neither old nor young—a fact in which you take some small, quadratic comfort.

> You: this red-dress-cotton body.
> You: this honey-wood box-life.

You've come to understand its contradictions.

> [What this means: you never think you smell nice when you don't]
>> [What this means: you know that scent is
>> far less shameful than a rip or hole—
>> than anything too hollowed
>> out and hungry]

III.

UNDER SATURN

My good hand trembles, groping for keys. Kitchen-filthy sneakers crunch against the film of ice coating the snow. I turn the key in the ignition. Press my bandaged hand against the steering wheel, fingers up, palm flat, middle finger throbbing under half a dozen Band Aides, under plastic poly gloves the chef and other line cook helped me layer once, then twice, then taped around the wound to keep it safe.

The engine rumbles to life, and with it something in my abdomen curls. The steering wheel feels foreign in my hand. I pull out from the curb outside the Blue Angel Café, past the windows—all still warm and flickering with light, with last-call drinkers at the bar—then on to Ski Run Boulevard. I recall the past three hours—hours on the clock, on the line, under pressure. Sweating under heat and yellow tickets as the Band Aides and the poly glove filled up with blood.

When I arrive back at the apartment, A opens the door. He looks at my hand, my face, then gently wraps his own long-fingered hands around my shoulders.

A is six-foot-four. I am five-foot-nine. Perhaps it shouldn't matter, but it does: the way his size seems to encompass me, despite the fact that he is touching just my arm, lifting just my left hand gently up to my right shoulder, fashioning a sling out of my paisley-printed thrift-store scarf. He does this—easily, methodically, with explanations [*elevate the wound; minimize disturbance*]. He is my first real boyfriend. Together, just last month, we bought a couch. He is twenty-nine years old. I am twenty-three. He has just retired from the military: given up his captain's rank in search of some new calling. So far, he hasn't found it yet. He has traveled six more years around this world than I have. I want this fact to justify, somehow, my relative weakness; make it safe for me to feel small. To tell him everything that happened—in the kitchen, on the line, the way my knife slipped, the way the orders kept coming, the way I kept working even as I felt my body flood with panic unequal to the danger of the wound—knowing he will understand. That none of it will scare him.

~ ~ ~

Finger anatomy is more complex than one might think. No muscles, for instance. Just a kind of pulley system: ligaments and tendons rigged to joint and bone. The musculature in charge belongs to palm and forearm. Another pulley system: each finger-motor-twitch beginning closer to the heart. Learning this, writing this, I'm drawn to look. To pulse and flex. Examine forearm, fingers, palm. My gaze lands on the middle finger—mine: long, insistent, brash. This fingertip holds things. It compels me to look closer.

Beneath the fleshy pad and half-moon middle fingernail, the structure binding things together—that is, the thing that makes a fingertip a tip—is called the distal phalanx. Distal, as in "situated away from the center of the body," away from "points of attachment." Anatomically, the middle finger is the *digitus medius*. More colloquially, it is the "long finger," "tall finger," or "the bird." In palmistry, it is called the "finger of Saturn." Depending on who's looking, its length might be measured to assess things like testosterone or penis size; risk of alcohol dependency or video game addiction; individual responsibility, discipline, or balance. It might be flipped upright against an otherwise curled fist to indicate *fuck you*. It might be fast to fracture in comparison to other fingers of the hand—especially in individuals with long and slender digits, like me.

And if one were to take this finger [of the left hand—mine, let's say] and make a proximal incision—cut towards the distal phalanx first, and ultimately aim the blade as if to bisect the entire finger like a hot dog bun—one might feel no pain. One might find one's self at a sudden distance, a state of remove from the action. One might wonder, then, at the source of this sensation: this odd crunch—like teeth on unexpected contact with an olive pit. First suppleness, then stone. One might wonder where the blood was even coming from, and marvel afterwards that none of it had smeared onto the bread, bread that one had been about to slice in half [a proximal incision, just like a hot dog bun, just now]. One might only start to feel the smart and sting and throb after inspecting it more closely: flap of flesh. Loose sole of a shoe.

The way it falls akimbo from all points of attachment.

And because *one* is, in this instance, *I*, she will find herself—months, years later—still inspecting this: her left-side Saturn finger. It's unmaking and remaking. The pink-white knitted skin. The ghost of half a half-moon scar, half-numb against her touch.

~ ~ ~

Saturn is a finger, is a planet, is a symbol, is a metal, is a sign. Here's what Saturn fingers mean—again, depending on who's looking; whose finger one is looking at, and why.

Saturn means authority or domination. It means method, obstinance, transition. It means labor or construction. It means power or stability. In Roman myth, Saturn was the god of—actually, it's hard to say. He was the god of many things: generation, dissolution, abundance, agriculture, time. He was the ruler of the so-called Golden Age.

A person, place, or thing that is *saturnine*—that is, "of Saturn"—might be dark, mysterious, or melancholic. In astrology, Saturn rules two signs, Aquarius and Capricorn. To fall under the sign of Saturn is to be more acutely influenced by the planet's associations. These include restriction, limitation, and self-control; boundaries of time, matter, and commitment; paternal influence and authority. Under Saturn, one is challenged to confront where she is from, where she might go—and what ultimately encircles, contains, and defines her life, her self.

As for me? My left-side Saturn finger is longer than its index by nearly half an inch. According to AuntyFlo.com [the veracity of which, perhaps, we should call into question], this means that I make "wise decisions." Stretch beyond the half-inch mark, however, and things get dark: "this leads to a conclusion that the person will meet their death through murder." So then. I measure and re-measure. I question the veracity of AuntyFlo.com [and measuring tape, and my eyesight]. I keep Googling. I find the website for Mark Seltman, a palmistry professional, who writes that those with dominant middle fingers are "frequently tall, slender, and angular in appearance;" that so-called "pure types" often have "dark hair, large bones, stern features, bland complexions." Seltman writes that bearers of such Saturn fingers might never get married. That they need space. That they might have trouble with their teeth. That they might be particularly organized, love classical music [violin or cello in particular—melancholic strings, a weakness]. That they lean satirical in terms of humor—but underneath their half-moon smirks, may also harbor deep feelings of obligation, obsessiveness, and self-critique.

I measure and re-measure. I examine my finger, its length, the grooves across my knuckles, the slight leftward tilt of the digit [the product of half a dozen bone fractures incurred during middle school basketball, a sporting phase inspired by my father's love of the game]. And so what if I am tall and pale and angular around the nose and collarbones? So what if I have fine brown hair and am slender—when I am busy, in particular, and find myself newly single after a January birthday [yes, Aquarius], newly grappling with solitude in a harsh and icy season? So what if I subsequently find myself standing at the kitchen counter, night after night, eating things like buttered toast and handfuls of arugula for dinner, then drinking bourbon neat? So what if I am home alone after putting on a reading series with my colleagues, only to be greeted at the door by bills for those three fillings I had done back in December—bills I'll likely forward to my father, sheepishly, because I just bought black leather boots I didn't need? And so what if I am now, at thirty-two, getting reacquainted with my solitude, finding myself half-lonely, half-relieved, listening to some vaguely familiar Vivaldi concerto on my little vintage wood-box radio as I write this, a smirk still lingering upon my lips from several paragraphs ago [as in, that bit where I referred to AuntyFlo.com and felt terribly superior to the internet and all its nonsense—].

I measure and re-measure. I inspect my half-moon Saturn finger scar. Who will tell me what it means for one to take this finger, all that it portends, and sever it? A proximal incision, aiming for the heart? Who will tell me what it means for one to take just such a severance—a loosening—and let it happen twice?

~ ~ ~

The second time it happens, I am ready.

The month is May, or it is October, or it is February.

That is, I'm in Los Angeles, so it is hard to tell.

I'm home alone, mincing garlic in the kitchen. There is shiny jet-black tile on the backsplash, terra-cotta tile underneath my long bare feet. A and I moved into this 1960s apartment complex off of

Sunset Boulevard back in November. A isn't home. I'm alone, and holding a chef's knife from Ross-Dress-For-Less. It was already cheap, and I got it even cheaper. I haven't sharpened it too recently, which I know is foolish—

    [that is, more dangerous than anything that's truly sharp]
    [that is, more dangerous than simply doing what I know
    I should]

It isn't that I don't have a sharpener. It's just that sometimes—after trying to hack three different freelance writing jobs, or working the busy lunch shift at a trendy Taiwanese café in Silver Lake, then battling droves of hipsters vying for a parking space at Trader Joe's, then lugging all the groceries upstairs and putting them away according to this strange refrigerator formula I've grown kind of attached to [and, quite frankly, would rather do alone and do it just the way I like], then showering and putting on a summer dress, then texting A to tell him that I'm starting to fix dinner and perhaps he should get home from whatever wandering [to the arcade or to the movie theater or to the Goodwill] that he's gotten up to by 7ish—sometimes, after all that, I get impatient. Waiting, I feel stuck. My fingers itch. And at this point, backtracking for the sake of something practical, like sharpening the blade, seems oppressive. Even though I know the satisfaction of resistance—first from carbide, then ceramic. Even though I know the pleasure of a sharpened blade—that newness chefs call "a factory edge."

And so, because I'm twenty-nine, and living in Los Angeles, and have a jet-black tile backsplash and real terra cotta tiles underfoot, and because I've worked at several restaurants since The Blue Angle

Café and am pretty confident, at last, that I can handle myself in
the kitchen [blasé, even, when it comes to blades and flames and
spitting oil, all barefoot, my dress some thing of flimsy cotton],
because I've poured a glass of wine already, started chopping onions
already, and would have to back up, change tack, re-wash the blade,
rummage through the drawers to find the sharpener, then dry the
blade—

—because of all this, I just keep mincing.

What's funny is the way the crunch, this time, feels almost friendly.
Like an echo. Familiar, the voice inside it mine. The severance, an
exhalation.

~ ~ ~

According to Roman myth, Saturn had two wives: Ops and Lua.
Ops was his second wife—the kind of woman that a god weds,
maybe, once he's grown into himself. Matured. Sowed his wild
oats, etc. Ops' name means "wealth, abundance, resources." As in,
something stable. As in, a good match.

I'm more interested in Lua. Her name means "destruction,
dissolution, loosening." Saturn wedded Lua first. I'll bet he was still
young then. Probably a total jerk, at times. Most likely, he cheated
on her in the end—or maybe even in the beginning. But I'd also
like to think that while they were in love, their love was wild.
Bloody. Bloody like the weapons Saturn and his warriors gave Lua

after coming back from war, each blade soaked with something vital from a fallen enemy. Something wet and real.

Lua has two nicknames: *Lua Saturni*—"Saturn's Lua"—and *Lua Mater*—"Mother Destruction." I don't care for either one. To me, they seem reductive. I'm more interested in her subtleties, her appetites. What was it that she really wanted—this woman who collected war-bent knives and swords as gifts? What more nuanced meaning might she have conceived for this, her moon-like name— *Lua*—

—as in, *loosening*?

~~~

Saturn is the ruling planet of Aquarians and Capricorns. But like any other planet, Saturn also moves. This means that everybody, every sign, falls under Saturn at one point or another.

One need only dabble superficially in matters of the zodiac to encounter the phrase, "Saturn Return." It's the kind of thing, one learns [especially when one has lived in California just a little bit too long] that certain people like to throw around in conversation. The Saturn Return is a so-called astrological transit, a phase in which the planet Saturn loops back to the same pocket of space in which it hovered at the moment of one's birth. The first such transit technically takes place for each and every one of us at twenty-nine-and-a-half years old—though, given the vast unmappable expanse of space and time and planetary motion, such a thing, by nature, must be inexact. That's why Saturn Returns are more often thought of, not so much as happening upon a certain day or year or season, but within a range of time: a window stretching roughly from twenty-seven to thirty-one.

No matter what one calls it, the first Saturn Return delineates a sea change. A reckoning: with what one knows, or thinks she knows, or wants to know about herself; with all the things one does not, in fact, know anything about at all.

I remember the first time I heard the phrase "Saturn Return." It was in a writing class [go figure], over wine and chips and introductions. We were in Los Angeles [go figure], Mount Washington to be exact. It was September, and I know that it was September, because that's when I signed up for the class—but also because of the peculiar effect of light and scent and temperature that rises from beneath the mountains up above San Bernadino, and the way the air would chill much more than I'd anticipate from week to week to week as August burned into October. I know that it was September because I'd finally learned to always bring a sweater.

Our class was held at the instructor's house—a funky, 1970s gem of a place with big windows and a deck and a flokati rug just like the one that A and I had purchased when we first moved to the city. I remember it was the smart, dry-witted Italian woman, a recent New York City transplant, who piped up as I introduced myself. I was twenty-nine, and getting ready to apply to graduate school, and

facing down the possibility of a long-distance relationship with A.
I said as much. That's when she interrupted me:

"Woman," she said—her voice was bold but kind, and she called
everybody *woman*—"woman, you are in your Saturn Return."

She went on to explain what this meant—or rather, I imagine that
she did. That is, I know she did in some way or another, but I can't
remember details. What I do recall is nodding; smiling; feeling
vaguely on the spot. Perhaps I wasn't even really listening. Perhaps
it wouldn't be until a little later that the significance of one's Saturn
Return would come to resonate; prompt me to remember.

But I didn't know that then.

And so I sat through class, and had another half-glass of wine, and
then put on my sweater and drove home to Silver Lake and looked
it up: *Saturn Return*. I tried to look beyond the HuffPost
summaries, every single one penned in the same voice and vein as
graduation cards; tried to push past countless critical analyses of No
Doubt's album, *Return of Saturn*. But after that, there wasn't much
to go on. All I really found—all that really stayed with me—was
this admonition: that approximately twenty-nine-and-a-half years
into one's life, one will, under sway of Saturn, either commit to her
current path, or else weigh anchor. Quit a job, leave a relationship,
move across the country. Sever ties, rupture expectations; cut loose
from all points of attachment.

~ ~ ~

Saturn's closest Greek equivalent is Cronus. The mighty Titan, son of earth and sky, frequently depicted with a knife, sickle, or scythe. Cronus used the scythe to castrate his father and usurp power. After that, he married his sister and they ruled as king and queen of the gods. Things were going pretty well for Cronus. Naturally, he wanted to prevent any major upset to his power, to the status quo. To keep things as they were, he ate his children. Of those children, only Zeus survived.

There are several different stories about what happened next. In one, Zeus slices Cronus through the stomach, freeing his snacked-on siblings in the process; in another, Cronus' wife Rhea cons him into swallowing a stone. Either way, Cronus gets his comeuppance. And really, in hindsight, practically anybody—even Cronus— could probably have seen this coming. Patricide, incest, cannibalism—it all adds up to the very definition of bad karma, or hamartia, or what have you, don't you think? Then again, who wouldn't be loath to sacrifice such power? Such a stable role, clear delineation of authority? Cronus, like Saturn, had ruled over a Golden Age. He'd had a good thing going. And while I wouldn't go so far as to condone his whole approach—to relationships, say, or parenting—I will confess: I can understand his motives.

~ ~ ~

I haven't cut myself in quite awhile. By cut, I mean *really* cut— ample bleeding, bandages, loose flaps of skin. By awhile, I mean about three years.

I want this fact to count for something. But does it? What does three years really mean, in the grand scheme of things? Can I get away with saying "it's been three years since I've really cut myself," and then say that I've learned? Evolved, somehow, in self-knowledge when it comes to limitations, to responsibilities?

Can I get away from this sneaking suspicion that some lessons, patterns, echoes, equations, might come in threes?

It's January. I live in Moscow, Idaho—a small town where things freeze in winter. It's been two years since I moved here for graduate school. Somehow, even though I drove all over Los Angeles, I still get anxious driving here—even at twenty-five mph—if there's ice. Anxious forcing gas and tires over muddied slush. I feel the same way about walking. Anytime there isn't enough traction, anytime I worry I might have to wait, or slip, or take the long way around, something in me flinches. Some slight nerve along my jaw. Not because I haven't done it since that first long winter down in South Lake [that is, driven—that is, walked]. Just because I get impatient sometimes, even though I know that I could practice more, move slower, strap on Yak Traks—

[this, by now, I know. That is, by now, I should]

But sometimes—after hustling my teaching life and grad school life into something that looks even remotely steady, after doing laundry and grading essays and writing essays and making sure my tights don't have enormous runs in them before I walk into my classroom, onto a stage in front of two-dozen eighteen-year-olds, my back and ass to them, my skirt continuing to ride up as I scribble things in dry-erase pen on the white board, things they'll never even bother to write down, and after hearing snickers while my back is turned and never knowing why [Was it my tights? My ass? Did someone pass a note? Do kids even do that anymore, or are they all just on their phones?], before then rushing to another class, then to lunch, then to class, then to post-class drinks, then to put my now-mildew-scented laundry in the dryer, then to stand still in the bathroom for a sudden moment and take more than one deep breath at a time and see the pinkish-purple half-moons underneath my eyes inside the mirror—sometimes, after all his, day in, day out, I'd rather not attempt to slice through one more thing.

That is, I'd rather not be quite so self-aware.

A and I broke up nearly a year ago. Now I'm dating someone else.

~ ~ ~

In palmistry, they say the left-hand side is what you're born with. All that you inherit. Origins and patterns. Things carried, things forgotten. I've never had my palm read, so I can't say too much more about it. All I know is this: my half-moon scar used to be white, and now it's pink. Or rather, it's invisible—blended deep into my skin—unless I look for it or startle myself now and then by looking when I do not mean to. Like when I'm in the shower, and the water's hot, and so my skin is hot and pink and something pinker suddenly stands out. Or when I look at my left hand, matched up against my right, and notice just how long my fingers are—so much longer than my mother's, so clearly like my father's—and then catch the hiccup in the pattern, cut deep into my left-hand middle finger. The red spots where they fray and spread apart.

My father is six-foot-four. Since I was a child, I've looked up to tall men. My father, when he shows physical affection, is primarily a hugger. When he hugs, he clings—encompassing, his size and weight around my shoulders and my ribs. My father rarely shows strong feeling through the more obvious channels—shouting, say, or tears. He has a relentless passion for his work, which is reinsurance litigation, trial presentation, precise and effective rhetorical maneuver. He is a sharp thinker, a devout procrastinator, and a perfectionist. I am not dissimilar.

My father fell in love with my mother, then fell back out. They met at the exactly right and fated time: when each wanted something stable, something workable, someone to have kids and buy a house with. My parents married when my dad was twenty-nine, my mom thirty-two. Not long after, my mom got pregnant. By my second birthday, I'm told, they'd already discussed divorce. My mother explains that Dad had strong feelings about divorce; that he told her, *Divorce is not an option. I don't want to only see my kid on weekends.* Hearing this as an adult, I wonder how much of this certainty came from a sense of duty—duty to romantic love lost but still honored, to parental love gained and overwhelming in its newness—and how much from a sense of performance. By performance, I mean appearances: the bounds of convention. Bounds that have taken me three decades myself to finally begin to question.

~ ~ ~

It is January. The last week of Winter Break at the university where my new boyfriend, B, and I both teach. B is twenty-nine. I'm almost thirty-two. We've been dating for nearly a year.

The sky is eyeball blue, the sun frost-white. Roads are slick. We are in my car. He is driving.

B is five-foot-ten at best, though if you ask, he'll tell you he is five-eleven. Perhaps it shouldn't matter, but it does—the way I wish him taller, want him to encompass me, somehow, and so I let him drive my car with ease and practiced hands. The way I give him lots of credit—as in, I try to trust him when he says he knows things. Things about philosophy [which he teaches], and wine [which he sells], and the Midwest [where he's from], and the Inland Northwest [which he loves], and himself. He is my second real boyfriend—as in, he bought me a toothbrush for the five nights every week that I sleep over; as in, his tiny gray-blue cat now knows the difference between me and other women.

Sometimes I forget that B is three years my junior; other times, it shows. B lives something of a charmed existence: stable job, lots of friends, lots of younger women who make it clear they'd like to date him. Like I said, ours is a small town; such things make themselves apparent—at the coffee shop, the bar, the alehouse, the redbrick restaurant where we always have our date nights. But the times when I am most smitten with B are those that challenge this—his ease, his stability. Times when he questions where he is, and what he's doing, and who he wants to be. I want the fact of this to mean more than it does: something about making him feel brave. If I'm being honest, I also want the fact of this to justify my weaknesses: the way I've started to ignore this jaw-nerve-flinch that happens often lately—verges into grinding, teeth on teeth, when I'm asleep. I want to let his generosity with wine and peanut butter toast, the way he loops his arms around me so tight in the morning, mean that I'm safe, somehow. Stable; held; defined as such—as a good match; as somebody worth holding. I want it to mean that I can relax, stop performing, just be honest, tell him everything.

Because sometimes, all I want is to slip out of the confines of my mind and blur into the beauty of an afternoon like this one: where it's Winter Break, and sun-bite-blue, and we are having what B calls "an adventure." Where we are, as he would put it, "being easy." This means snowshoes and a short hike and an afternoon of sandwiches and beer. Snowshoes that we aren't even quite sure how to fasten or walk in, that we wear even as they slip and lurch beneath us, even as we blunder over drifts—because there isn't any rush. Because it's not like we're trying to get somewhere. Sandwiches and chips and beer at 2PM because there's no reason why not—and anyway, we weren't even awake until 11AM because it's Winter Break, and so we stay up late for bedtime sex and wake up late for morning sex and tumble into sex on Sunday afternoons [like we'll probably do when we get home, the curtains only half-way drawn, the whiteout snowfall mirroring the whiteness of our white-pale winter bodies].

After lunch, we wander into an antique store seeking treasure. B is very fond of this word: *treasure.* As in, I bring him oranges, or organic bagels from the local bakery, or a pack of Trident gum—the green kind—and he says, "What treasures!"

Sometimes I find this more obnoxious than endearing. Sometimes I wish that he would just grow up. Sometimes I worry I've become a snob.

Then again, there is some charm to this—B's gift for whimsy. So we go inside. And what I end up purchasing surprises me. It's a pocketknife: vintage, slim, petite. Marbled handle, flimsy blade, red and cream and chrome. The knife is small enough to fit inside that useless micro-pocket someone opted to squeeze in, sub-hipbone, underneath the belt loop of my so-called skinny jeans. The knife is light and feels more like a talisman than a tool. But I've never owned a pocketknife of any kind—never purchased any blade that wasn't for the kitchen.

It's pretty. Rectangular, with gently rounded edges.
It feels good in my hand.

B leans in close as I approach the register. Flashes me a smile. I look down at his hands: his short, even, sturdy fingers. His uniformly bitten nails.

I half-moon smile back.

~ ~ ~

Two days later, I am standing in my kitchen. I'm alone. I pry the thin and rusted blade out from the marble case of red and cream and chrome. Underneath its pretty case, the steel's slim edge is duller than a nail file. Weaker than a butter knife. I'm disappointed, but I try it anyway. Partially because I've been flipping through this very silly-but-enticing book, *How To Be Parisian Wherever You Are*, [as in, how to cultivate an air of gravitas and mystery even if you live in Idaho; how to drink champagne with ice cubes in it so you won't get too drunk at the party; how to wear navy blue on black and make it work; how to seem as if you have a secret lover even though you don't—even though you never have].

In this book, they say to score the soles of brand-new heels or boots. They say to cut them with a sharp knife for more steadiness, more traction. I am a fast walker. By now, everyone in town knows this about me. B knows, in particular. B is always asking me to *please slow down*. But I like to walk fast; like to weave between the slower-moving crowds in cities, or on Farmer's Market days. I value traction. I value mobility. But I've also just received these brand-new leather boots in the mail. Boots I ordered for myself, a kind of early birthday present, on a discount New Year's clearance [still expensive], on my credit card. They are fancy boots: impractical and sleek, but very pretty.

So I use my fingernails to pry the blade free from its case of red and cream and chrome. And even though I'm not quite sure how best to twist or aim the blade—how to sever past the slick-sheen-plastic surface of the soles without destroying these, my new and pretty shoes—I press the knife down anyway.

THE NEED TO USE YOUR TEETH

El Niño storms are eating up the sand of California's coast,
wet bite by bite. Think of the ocean as a body diseased—
turning in upon its shores, ravenous and swollen.
Gnawing at the sand like skin. Gnawing
at the flecks of other little bodies—
corals, mollusks, reefs—
rendered pink or white or black,
peppered over with volcanic glass. Gnawing
at the borders of its own capacious body.
The hypnotherapist had two small dogs, white terriers.
The more outgoing one always pressed his hot, squirming body
up onto my lap as I tried to lean back and relax, week after week,
in the beige pleather recliner. *Lean back and relax*, he'd say,
even though it felt like something charged was moving
through my body—something electric, something
I could not release. *Anxiety is energy*, he'd say, his voice a murmur,
Nutella-thick, behind my shuttered eyes. *You are letting it consume you.*
You are eating yourself. The skin along my neck prickled
and rose; I felt a swelling at my throat.
What is it that you aren't allowed to do? To say?

Throat swollen to the point of shut—shut-up.
Ask yourself: why this hunger? Why the need to use your teeth?
Lesch-Nyhan syndrome (LNS) is an endocrine disorder produced
by gene mutations to the X chromosome. These mutations warp
the body's uric acid balance—a balance normally maintained
by kidneys, by the way they cleanse the blood. In turn,
the LNS-afflicted body loses other forms of balance:
fluid levels, kidney function, neurological stability.
Such bodies, thus disrupted, turn cannibal.
As children, patients with LNS begin to bite and chew
their lips and fingers, to experience involuntary or compulsive
motion of the limbs. Strange appetites; unbidden flails.
Nearly all recorded cases of full-fledged LNS occur in males.
But there are milder cases—less serious, less obvious—
and these can occur anywhere, in any body.
I started biting young. Age three, or maybe four.
The inside of my lower lip, the plump smooth flesh against
my cheek, the soft tissue up against my nails and cuticles. Nicks
and bites to peel off flecks of pink-white skin. A nervous habit.
Nervous, as in: edgy, jumpy, skittish, brittle, tense. Nervous, as in:
the Latin *nervosus* for sinewy, vigorous. Vigor, as in *energy*.
Dynamic. Powerful. The boundaries of skin
perhaps too fragile, too unstable
to fight back.
Coasts, as boundaries between land and water,
are characterized by the geologic nature of the land,
which is unstable and often fragile, and the dynamic power of wind

and sea. As a result, coastal environments are constantly changing
as they seek to achieve and maintain equilibrium
among the many opposing natural forces[1].
This hunger ebbed and flowed.
Sometimes all I needed was a gentle pressure:
teeth against my lip. Other times it soaked me through:
this need, the gnawing. The hunger brimmed within me,
coursing vein and muscle, compelling hands to rise and press,
telltale, against the mound of cheek curved soft above my jaw.
I was ashamed. I felt diseased. I wanted to know *why*
as much as he did when, twenty-odd years later, I asked for help:
body stuck against the pleather, warm damp of terrier breath
against my palm. I wanted to know if there were others like me—
anxious cannibals—turning in upon their shores.
Wanted to know so I could ask them:
why this hunger? Why the need to use your teeth?
A body is a storm-gnawed ocean.
A body is volcanic nerves and pink-sand skin,
wet tongue, and teeth as sharp as glass.
A body out of whack reveals pathologies.
A body builds up waste when something can't get *out*.
A body is a thing of unknown hungers.
A body is an ocean is a swelling
is a sickness is a hunger is a swelling

---

[1] "Coastal Erosion and Land Loss Around the United States: Strategies to Manage and Protect Coastal Resources," by S. Jeffress Williams, USGS, Coastal and Marine Geology Program. August 2001.

is a throat that's swelling, swollen full
against the portcullis
of glass white teeth—
and then
it shuts.

CRAMPING AT THE BONE

You[1] tell me [now, outside the bar, tonight, as we are leaning each against the roughened brick, as you are smoking and I run my tongue along my drying lips] this thing about the subject of the sentence. As in, my sentences keep lacking them. This thing: the subject [lacking].

~ ~ ~

At this, my body slips. Slides a little down and sideways, wondering. I tilt my eyes; my head. Yours are steady, but your fingers and the orange, burning endpoint of your Camel menthol quiver in the windless, moon-blue dark. That is: your body, likewise, slips. This is natural. This is how a body works. A body sprawls, multiple in all its makings and

---

[1] Perhaps a single person. Perhaps several. Perhaps, at times, myself—or even you. Or even language, how it slips. Let these options coexist; let them multiply and blur.

unmakings. But what I want to know is what's left over [under?]: what, within a body, holds? Not the legs or fingers, or the kind of hair like mine that scatters[2], windswept, any volume an artifice [powders, brushing, barrel irons]—not, that is, the hair itself. Unpacked, it all falls flat. Even bone because a bone can thin and hollow.

~ ~ ~

I don't know how to tell you what I mean. I bum a drag instead.

~ ~ ~

The word *subject* comes from the Latin *subjectus*—meaning, "brought under." A line break, or an indent, or a footnote, leaps and pushes language underneath. But what about *brought*—that is, the bringing: two hands carrying or pulling, moving meaning laterally

---

[2] Extremities do not hold and press, insist on weight, the way the center of a body does. If I want to hold you, I could try to use my lips, my hands; but if I wanted to make sure you *stayed*, I would need more force. Lay my body down against you.

from one place to another? The difference has to do with carriage as opposed to energy and text that presses as it piles. Either way, I end up focused on accumulation; weight. What I feel within the confines of a tighter space: tiny, urgent shifts within the cracks, between the brick. But does it follow, then, that breakage *brings*? Does it *carry*? I don't know. I don't think so, necessarily. What's true is that a breakage is overt—that it calls out, draws attention with each reaching arm.

~ ~ ~

For the sake of this, right now, tonight—the moon, the brick, the hint of menthol on my tongue, the way it lingers, how you let your cigarette just rest and stick along your lazy upper lip, how it makes me want to kiss you— let's imagine you and I are lovers. Let's imagine, at the very least, we were.

~ ~ ~

The notion of the subject lends itself to much confusion. Consider: SUBJECT[3]: as brought under, thrown beneath; as the primary figure under scrutiny or discussion; as the grammatical element around which the rest of a clause is predicated, or the central part of a proposition; as a leading theme or motif, or a branch of knowledge; as subordinate; as the conscious mind or ego, especially as opposed to anything external to the mind—that is, the central substance of a thing as opposed to its attributes; the thing inside the [body] thing itself, that which MAKES that thing a "self"[4]; as dependent or conditional upon, or under the authority/thumb of [____]; to cause or force to undergo; to bring—a country, or a person, or a notion, language, text—under control. Consider my subjective role; my authority as the digester of established codes, as borrower of language, definition [sometimes copying verbatim from the purported facts of language—what a word does, indubitably, mean—and sometimes skewing my translation just a little bit, making cuts, adding a word, subtracting several, embracing the non-historic, non-factual, hole-ridden, angular refraction of the facts].

---

[3] Oxford English Dictionary

[4] This particular definition seems as if it might—or should—resolve the matter. But, as you can see, the definitions continue; they sprawl.

~~~

And maybe let's imagine I am writing you a letter. Let's imagine you are not right here, standing in the cooling night beside me [reaching; ache; this micro-distance in between our bodies, how it reaches, grows inside my chest the more I wait and stand and look at you, your lips, your steady gaze—]

~~~

Or perhaps I started out to write a poem. To find the inside stuff beneath the surface, packed and filling up the middle of the thing. Perhaps I started out determined: *stay right here.* Feel into this box, its tightness, short and quickened breath. As if I were an airplane passenger en route to L.A. from New York, stuck with nothing but this body and these hands for hours—five or six—it has been years since I have made this kind of trip, and now in fact I realize I have *never* flown from L.A. to New York, that I am writing fiction, or perhaps a poem after all because a poem never promised to be true—and how a box of language, when one can't climb out, or punch a hole somewhere, or verge into a corner, might in fact force one to stretch the way I stretched the first time I took yoga in my freshman year of college, vowed to fold in half each day and night and day until my fingers reached beyond the stiffness of my hamstrings, glutes, and calves down to my toes; that is, turned my too-long, scattered body and its separateness into a single circuit—closed.

~ ~ ~

Then again, perhaps what I mean to say is less about my love for you—less about this "you" and "me," less about these bricks and lips and summer nights—and rather something vague and bothersome about the sentence. How a sentence moves. Its processes and turns. About my love affair with sentences [or you]. About the infidelity of lines. About the urge I've felt, so often in the summertime, to break—

~ ~ ~

—or else, more recently, to stay: remain inside. Like sentences, the urges also turn. Sometimes with the weather. The colder brittle leaves appear, swirling and cracking on the pavement, the more I want to stay inside. I will admit to loving gray: especially the mornings, how they stretch sometimes into the night. How sometimes, all day long is purple-gray and white, and brittle leaves until the sunset comes: a burst of shouting pink and gold against the backdrop of the end. There are days when sun without the privacy of warmth—the silent melt of lying on the carpet in a pool of it or lying *by* a pool [with almost-silent chlorinated blue, without the screams of children or the eyes of men] is more like an assault. Sunlight is a gaze. Sunlight *insists;* subjects my body to its blazing. My instinct is to battle this. With gray, I can remain inside or outside as I choose, my body free to spread beneath thick sweaters, blending in, unnoticed as it moves, held and loose at once against my black-white-box-check coat, against a sea of black-coat bodies, boxed and walking fast with short, black steps.

~ ~ ~

Now you will say *this is not a poem.* This is a wandering. An attempt. It is an essay, or at least pieces of one. Except that I am trying [as much as I can] not to break this subject into pieces. I am trying to stay put. It may not seem like it—

despite the ruse of form—because this volume, this solidity, is artifice. With time and wear, it thins. It breaks. You can see it very easily—you have only to look down. I can see it, too. Like I said: artifice. But it is also something like necessity. It is difficult to be inside the body. I do not like it here unless I am succumbing to the circuitry—the looping energy—of breathless run-ons. I like to fall down into language, but my body does not like to fall and that is why I do not ski or roller blade or ride a bike. I like to think I know the difference. Then again, who's to say each block of text, so long as it propels and turns, is not also a poem? Is not also a fiction, or the truth?

~ ~ ~

The bone of my left upper canine is recessed. Thinning out, like glass. If I could make my body small and crawl inside the hollow of my mouth, examine where the twist and curl of speech is coming from [behind the teeth, behind the tongue], I might get close enough to see something of gum and cheek—to peer behind the thinning bone, the pink of flesh—towards the root. Root is *nerve*; is *brain* [yet even synapse, fiber, nerve—all of it is still the body]. Would I sacrifice the solidness of bone in order to see past all this—to see inside my mind, crawl further still, grow smaller, shrink and grind my body down—reduce the definition of a body to its smallest point? Would this smallness, in its distillation, be a thing that holds?

~ ~ ~

I am a serial writer and re-writer of lists. If this is artifice, it is also not a secret. My days, then, become these structured texts: one after another. Structure gives me comfort. You know this all too well. So then, if I'm trying to push boundaries, what is the opposite? Is the answer dreams? If I am the subject of the dream, what is the dream itself? In the dream, I am at once author and subordinate. In the dream, I am thrown beneath my mind and day and drowsiness. The dream is not my text, per se. But it is also solely mine, without external author, without any translation offered or available beyond that which I might attempt [or eschew]. Inside the inside of my mind: that is where a dream is written. The dreams: they turn like sentences. They take different forms. The dreams unpack themselves within a box of sleep. It is a large box. Some nights, it fills. The dreams: they sprawl, multiplicitous in my unmaking. The body [mine] can't get out from under them. The mind is curled and caught beneath their weight and bend—that is, brought under. If I am thus the subject of my dream, what is the dream itself? A breakage? Slipping skin? A paradox? A kind of gray?

~ ~ ~

Let's imagine you are absent. That even as you stand here, close to me, I [already?] miss you. Want to tell you what it is I love [about your lips and hands and eyes—sea glass, ever steady up above the curling smoke]. What I love is how you tell me things about myself without insisting that you know—who I am entirely, that is, or who I ought to be. The way you offer me myself as subject—not to be *brought under* [you], but to remind me that I have two hands and many shovels and am very capable of digging. Like me, you are a close reader. You observe the tension that creeps up between the cracking bricks. You catch my tics—like when I look down and to the right instead of making eye contact[5]. You smile in a very certain way when my head tilts, when my mind strays: from

[5] This is absolutely true. You have even seen me do it. In person, even on the page [that is, *indent?*]

this [the night, the blare of streetlamps]. You say: *you are such an essayist.* You catch me in my multiplicities. You take away my footnotes, all my scattered narratives. You do not put me in a box. Instead, you hand it to me: put the box between my cold red hands. What I hear you say—what I want to hear, and so I do—is this: *HERE. MAKE. STAY UNTIL IT LOOKS LIKE SOMETHING TRUE.*

~~~

Perhaps this is what it means: *to fall.* If I fall asleep, and in my sleep I write the text of dreams, and then I wake and write as straight and bare as I can stand to write, write to catch each image, movement, my sole subjective move the faultiness of memory...well, what is the difference? What, in fact, do I know? Perhaps what I like to think, and what I think, and what I know [that is, posses, hold, like an object in my palm, like the inside of the inside of myself, like the text between these brackets, or your hands, your love that I have slipped and fallen hard beneath]—perhaps all of these are separate things, indeed. Disparate, even as they overlap.

~ ~ ~

I am trying to make sense of our affair. My attraction has to do with how you seem to care less about the answer than the push—than me, moving [under?][6]. Even if that means I move farther from you. Or further inside myself. Even if it means pressing my body down—hands reaching, gripping, torso curled in half to close the circuit—rather than my body flung against yours in the dark. And even as I squirm and want to branch off into other stories, linkages, even as I twist and crack my neck against the confines of the sitting, making, digging [more into the core of something hidden, something seeded, than beneath the ground or underneath my nails, my skin, sprawling like an itch], I am in love with you. How you make me want to see myself this way—alone, and still.

~ ~ ~

If imagining your absence frightens me—even now, tonight, even as I feel it coming, feel this

---

[6] Almost as if you were an essay—an attempt—

distance growing—it also, somehow, soothes. Knowingness and absence may go hand in hand. That is, knowing isn't possible; but knowing is not the locus of agency. The seed of knowing might become a thing, a text, which, through language, I can give you—put into your hands [or mine] to hold. But it is also irreducible to any single point [body—seed—truth—self]. In this, our multiplicities will always be eluding one another. This is absolutely true. Absence is true. All these angles for it—ways of breaking, digging, at the thing itself, fully worked out, and the main room at the center, until what's left is many smaller rooms, each a different doorway to ambivalence[7]. To cracks and open spaces. Gaps for ghosts. For dreams. Incomprehension and suggestion. You might say: *choose the room that trips you—interrupts your sense of knowing anything at all. Lose control. Let the room, the cage, the risk and its uncertainties, arrest you*[8].

---

[7] After Anne Carson.

[8] The original—body, story, lover, myth, yourself, myself—does exist. It is in the center. But you are not. I am not. We are underneath. The original is X. We cannot solve for X. And so, instead, we say: HERE. STAY. MAKE. YOU MUST RENAME IT.

DEPTH CONTROL

It is a rainy afternoon in late October. I am dressed for it: tight black jeans, black Salvation Army mock-neck polyester sweater, sleek-black coat. My favorite leather boots—heel-strike worn, the wood abraded at a slant—click against the dampened pavement.

By *it*, I mean the weather, but also, the tattoo. My first. The sweater's particular shade of nearly-black, its 1970s vintage, signal [to my mind, at least] a suitable equation: poise and thrift and subtle edge; sleeves just loose enough to roll above the elbow.

It is a Tuesday. After the tattoo, I will attend a lecture with a visiting writer. I will sit in a black-box theater in my black mock-neck sweater and prepare something articulate to say when asked for feedback. Underneath the sweater, the skin of my right forearm will prickle, smart, and redden.

But I won't know what that feels like until later. Until then—before the smart, before the theater—I am here. Unmarked, and walking.

I listen to the speed and measure of my heels against the sidewalk. I wait for the traffic light to turn, hang left in front of Wells Fargo, turn right into the alley off Third Street. I enter the tattoo parlor from a whitewashed wooden door. I turn the brass doorknob, step out of the rain-slick street, feel the warmth of yellow lamplight pouring through the un-screened windows. The hour is high noon. The darkness of the day makes it seem later.

I shake the rain off my umbrella, my coat, and scuff my boots against the doormat, then walk across the cream and orange patterned floor, past the black ceramic cathead cocked to the side, yellow eyes following me, sidelong. I perch along the edge of this: minute, hour, brown crushed-velvet couch. Above me, the roof is silver aluminum; around me, the walls are red brick, peppered with framed prints: cave paintings, 70's flowers in a vase, *Star Trek's* Mr. Spock, phaser out, rendered in neon pastel-on-cardboard. To my right, a heavy wood reception counter sports dried flowers, a dark blue globe, a deer skull painted gold.

I'm excited. I'm nervous as fuck.

I'm here alone, by design. Last night, B left a card on my doorstep—a note of encouragement, a promise to buy me a celebratory drink afterwards. I appreciated the gesture, but found it unnecessary—grasping, even. I wasn't having second thoughts. Hadn't been since August, back when my California license plates expired and A had called to explain how he'd failed to forward my registration forms in time to legally renew without excessive fees, back when I'd found myself at the Latah County DMV—a single room with clean gray carpet and two sweet old ladies working the desk and only one person ahead of me in line, a place unrecognizable as a DMV after Downtown Los Angeles, after the massive gray cement compound with its numbered service stalls, endless lines, cheerless staff, terrifying parking lot. I'd found myself fingering the free literature, then examining the custom Idaho license plates, wildlife-themed, available for purchase. I could opt for bluebird, elk, or trout. The plates were $35 each, and proceeds went to nature conservancy programs on the Palouse. I looked, and I considered. I liked the elk but felt no affinity for it. For a moment, I reconsidered the $200 it would take to keep my white plates, blue numbers, cheesy red-loop script—*California*. Something in my throat filled up.

So what I mean to say is this: the card was something of a reach. Then again, the tattoo artist is a friend of B's, and this acquaintanceship gives me some small comfort. Like insurance: security against unsteady hands or careless harm. This is what I'm thinking as I sit here now, perched, too nervous to lean back into the plush. All my senses are on fire. I notice that it's warm inside. I notice that it smells good: not chemical or sterile, but sweet and slightly woody—palo santo, maybe, mixed with something richer and more feminine. The light, too, is warm and soft. Something groovy on the stereo. Since I'm killing time, I ask: *Surf's Up*, The Beach Boys, 1971.

The tattoo parlor is familiar in a distant sort of way. I've been here twice—first for a poetry reading, then for my initial consultation. But today is different. Today, from noon to two [or whenever we are finished—that's the length of my appointment], I'm here and only here. I breathe it in: the orange, cream, and velvet brown; the black ceramic cat, the woody sweetness. Today I want it all inside of me, underneath the skin.

What are the chances of it going wrong?

I'd asked, back in September. In reply, the artist had stretched both his thick and woody forearms out towards me, palms up, displaying half a dozen different images—a dinosaur, a sparrow, a weeping Madonna—all inked in hues of charcoal gray or deep black-green, pronounced against the bourbon of his skin.

You think that I'd keep doing this if it were high?

My skin is sensitive. I bruise easily, flush quickly. I've never done well with extremes. When it comes to wounds, I'm risk averse. I want to understand my vulnerabilities. I told the artist all of this, more or less: after I'd shown him countless images of Western Cypress trees [*Cupressus macrocarpa* a variety of chaparral native to the California coast]; after he'd enlarged my favorite photograph— a wide-stretched, old grove stunner from Point Lobos—then fattened the trunk, funked up the branches, and applied a stencil twice the size I'd asked for to the inside length of my right forearm. The stencil ink was loud. A dankish purple, abrupt against the pink-white of my skin.

Together, we'd admired and critiqued my new reflection in the mirror as I rotated my arm outwards, then inwards, examining the way the branches reached towards my wrist bone, the way the skin and fascia moved in concert with a ghostly wind. I wore the purple stencil on my forearm until it faded. Then I made the appointment for today's tattoo: the real thing.

I'm not left waiting long. The artist is prompt. He calls me back behind the wooden counter, back to the corner of the studio where he sits at a drafting table, then pulls up the image of my cypress on his desktop. We don't know each other well, and every time he laughs—loud, wide-open mouth, all teeth—I struggle to take him seriously. But watching him work, I notice different things. How tall he is, for instance. Eyes big and dark; rich brown hair; thick beard. Italian, perhaps, or Greek, the way his skin is always golden brown. A sometimes brand of handsome. I notice the arsenal of chemicals as he sets them out: gentian violet, Dettol, green soap, ink. The smooth-cold feeling as he rubs my forearm clean, then presses down the final stencil: a tri-branched cypress, roughly four inches long, roots aligned with the ulnar side of my wrist, branches reaching from my elbow-crease [that sensitive and vein-rich nexus that tattooers call "the ditch"] towards my flexor tendon. When he isn't working at the tattoo shop, the artist draws portraits and pinups: Lauren Bacall, Marlena Dietrich, Rita Hayworth. He works in charcoal, pencil, and pastel. The Spock portrait, I learn, is one of his—the cardboard medium, a signature. Now he's pulling on bright blue latex gloves, and I'm nervous-talking, asking questions about art school as he lines up tiny cups like thimbles, each brimming with black or gray ink, a scoop of Vaseline swathed out with a tongue depressor, a stack three inches deep of torn-off paper towels. I tell him about my parents' love of early *Star Trek* episodes, about how much my mom would love the portrait. We laugh. He takes up the electric needle; removes the sterile plastic cap.

When it comes to wounds, I'm curious. About the cost. About the different routes we take to sturdiness. Tattoos and immunity rely on one another. The minute a needle touches flesh, armies of macrophages are deployed to eat the ink. Fibroblasts race to soak it in, to keep the dermis from transforming. But the cells remain suspended in the dermal layer, their efforts in defense against the ink serving only to ensure its survival. A tattoo, then, is less an act of writing *on* the body, of scarring the surface, and more a means by which to crawl beneath—that is, go under; get inside.

Following instructions, I lie down on the table. The artist sits to my right. I press my booted feet down into soft black pleather, turn my head to the left, just like I always do when getting blood drawn. I'm looking for distractions. There are plenty: whitewashed shelves bedecked with geodes, succulents sprouting out of seashells, a long-dead bat preserved beneath a dome of glass.

Okay, here we go, he says.

We are starting with the trunk. I inhale sharp. The needle whirs. I look away. He scratches the first thin line—gnarled and erupting from a mound of coastal rock—into my arm. I turn my head towards him once again, and there it is. The ink. Except that now, the ink's a branch. Indelible. The ink, the tree: no longer each to each.

At first, I scarcely feel it, so caught up am I in all of this observing. But as the work—the whirring, buzzing, scratching—continues, I find myself drawn closer in: to the sensation, to the bend and curl of pain. I grow curious about the difference: between what I experience, lying here, subject to the needle, and what it's like to stitch into the pattern of a stranger's skin.

How is it different for you than drawing with a pencil? I ask.

For one thing, the artist begins, *a pencil stops when pressed against a sheet of paper.*

This answer gives me pause. I am compelled; I am afraid. I reel my mind back from its customary wandering—association, definition.

This takes effort. The effort seems well worth it.
What I mean is this: for once, it seems wiser not to wonder what a needle does when pressed.

Soon, it becomes difficult to separate the literal sensation of the needle from the sound. Sever what is happening between the epidermal and the dermal layers of my skin from that telltale clatter in my ears—mechanized and violent, like an electric sewing machine mated with a lawn mower. I lie there, face upturned towards the silvery aluminum, and try—before the feeling grows familiar, before the shock of newness dissipates—to find the words for what it feels like. Try to do away with hearsay associations [like what B had said—*it's like a bunch of little beestings*], keep my mind from drifting into worry, into tangents, and stay present with my skin, my nerves. Every pinch and tingle. I watch the artist's blue-gloved hand in my periphery. I try to notice what he smells like, but I can't. Even with him leaning over me, his body so close to mine, the Dettol and the wood-sweet incense and the musk of my own perfume-muddled sweat have taken over. Instead, I will the sound, the whirr, to leave my consciousness. I recall being a little kid in school: drawing on my hands, with ballpoint pen. And I realize, in fact, that's exactly what this feels like: a pen. Very sharp, ultra-fine, razor precise. No cushioned rollerball. A sharp pen pressed beyond the surface of the skin, past the point where many times before I've jotted notes or names or meeting reminders, bereft of Post-Its, along the tender flesh between my pointer knuckle and the big joint of my thumb.

So ultimately, it's a matter of mastering depth control.

The artist says this as he works: beyond the outline, into the shading and the contours, the contrast and the patterning of gray against the black. As I begin to grow accustomed to this scratching, to the variations in the pain—now superficial like a sharpened fingernail, now deep and vibratory like a Brillo pad. As I finally grow bored looking away, and turn, instead, to watch. Watch the stark black ink embedded, line by line, stroke by stroke, beyond the peach-pale sheath that holds my body closed. Watch the gray ink filling in: foliage and shadow. *Depth control.* The phrase sticks with me. In spite of myself, I can feel the mental gears shifting and buzzing, the morning's adrenaline morphing now into something not unlike a caffeine high, but deeper, better; a sort of intellectual arousal that occurs whenever I'm struck by the seed of a really neat idea. Usually, I'm alone at my desk, or at the coffee shop, or walking briskly when this happens—when my body floods with sudden energy, with a rush of sapiosexual horniness, and I want to somehow write and fuck and drive over the speed limit all at once, all at the same time. I don't, of course. I stay inside my head, or write things down. I walk faster, or break into a run, or go get a beer. Usually, I just push through the moment and the rush, then talk to an imagined audience later on that night, naked, in the shower, letting heat and wet run over me until my skin turns red, until the feeling dulls.

But this feeling, now, under the needle, is a different feeling. More satisfying, in the sense that I am trapped. Even as my mind is buzzing, looping, it returns right back again to this—to needle, Dettol, palo santo, skin. A tiny circuit, tight and hot. Nothing left to do but lie here, still, and feel it.

The needle moves. It bites. It fills. Sometimes, I wince. Sometimes, I feel like I am getting a massage. Time passes. Sooner than I would have thought, the artist is putting the finishing touches on the reaching branches. I'm watching, and I'm feeling, and I'm thinking things about infection and erosion, about biting in, and wearing down. Now that it's nearly over, I free myself to think beyond this: minute, hour, forearm, present. To consider depth, and pencils, paper—what the artist's hands might feel like on my skin without those stupid rubber gloves. Or what would happen if the needle sunk too far: where it might land, and where the ink would go, and what's beneath all this.

Depth. The word suggests a destination. The surface of the ocean to its floor. Or distance measured, quantified—as in, *the needle penetrates my skin to a depth of 1mm.* Feelings can be deep: incomprehensible and tiny in their truths, like the strange affinity I felt with that dead bat beneath the glass when I stood close enough to see its jaw propped open in a death scream or a yawn, its tiny canines smaller than my half-moon Saturn finger scar. Depth is a gradation of color. Like the effect of rendering and shadow, the effect of light yielding to dark, gray ink to black, the knobby elbow of a branch made real as mine with the right contrast and intensity. Or else it is some darkness—some unknown thing inside that no one sees. My body, for example: underneath the skin, right now, as I am sitting up and the artist is tidying the weeping edges—seeping fluid, bloody trace—then giving me a spiel about Saniderm, the bandage he adheres over the fresh tattoo.

The Beach Boys' "Feel Flows" is playing on the stereo. My right forearm throbs with heat. On the inside, immunity is kicking in already. Pressing back against the biting and the plumbing, against the newly married ink and skin. On the outside, I am smiling and saying *thank you*. I am gathering my things, pausing for a moment to roll up my sleeve, examining the gnarled roots, the fishhook branches, the way the textured foliage reaches and warps as if imbued with salt and wind.

I swipe my credit card in the machine, taking quick note of the time: *1:38PM*. I sign the digital receipt like this: my finger, just a single curl of black. I scoop the bucket of my green knit hat over my hair and snap the buttons of my coat. And then I turn my back, and turn the handle of the door, and open my umbrella to the rain.

ACKNOWLEDGEMENTS

I'm grateful to the journals where selections (in some form or another) from this manuscript first appeared: "Indentations" in *Sonora Review*; "[This Body] Fictions" in *Third Coast*; "Madonna of the Master Bath" in *FENCE*; "Bruxisms" in *DIAGRAM*; "Dark Storage" in *Indiana Review*; "That Same Summer" in *Ninth Letter*; "On Shame" in *The Pinch*; "Cramping at the Bone" in *Denver Quarterly*; "The Need to Use Your Teeth" in *The Baltimore Review*, and "Depth Control" in *Phoebe*.

Thank you to the readers and mentors who helped usher the first drafts of this project into the world, in particular Kim Barnes, Brian Blanchfield, Alexandra Teague, and Sarah VanGundy. Much appreciation to my MFA cohort and professors at the University of Idaho, to my teachers and friends from the WWLA days (Margaret Wappler, Chris Daley, Kim Young, Jessica Ripka, Andrea Ciannavei), and to my long-ago Tin House workshop compatriots (Sarah Ciston, Tonya Canada, Christopher Gaumer, and Mary-Kim Arnold). I am indebted to so many authors and thinkers who influenced my work on this book, as well—both directly as teachers and indirectly as writers whose books I devoured again and again—including Maggie Nelson, Bhanu Kapil, Kazim Ali, T Fleischmann, Anne Carson, Sarah Vap, Aisha Sabatini Sloan, Joan Didion, Claudia Rankine, Renee Gladman, Kate Zambreno, Arianne Zwartjes, and others.

LAUREN W. WESTERFIELD

Sincere thanks to the editors at Unsolicited Press for taking a chance on this strange manuscript and giving the book a home.

Lastly, love and thanks to my mother and father. And of course, to A, B, and C—for the memories, stories, fragments of a life.

ABOUT THE AUTHOR

Lauren W. Westerfield is a writer from Northern California. She teaches at Washington State University, where she serves as Editor-in-chief of *Blood Orange Review,* and lives in Spokane, Washington.

ABOUT THE PRESS

Unsolicited Press is based out of Portland, Oregon and focuses on the works of the unsung and underrepresented. As a womxn–owned, all–volunteer small publisher that doesn't worry about profits as much as championing exceptional literature, we have the privilege of partnering with authors skirting the fringes of the lit world. We've worked with emerging and award–winning authors such as Shann Ray, Amy Shimshon–Santo, Brook Bhagat, Kris Amos, and John W. Bateman.

Learn more at Unsolicitedpress.com. Find us on Twitter and Instagram at @UnsolicitedP.

www.ingramcontent.com/pod-product-compliance
Lightning Source LLC
Chambersburg PA
CBHW020442040225
21364CB00008B/89

* 9 7 8 1 9 5 6 6 9 2 9 4 5 *